THE

Maria Thun
BIODYNAMIC
CALENDAR
2022

CREATED BY
MARIA AND MATTHIAS THUN

Floris
Books

Floris Books is proud to be part of the international biodynamics movement. We aim to support biodynamic farmers, small-holders, wine-makers and gardeners by publishing informative and inspiring books, calendars and apps.

Compiled by Titia and Friedrich Thun
Translated by Bernard Jarman
Additional astronomical material
by Wolfgang Held and Christian Maclean

Published in German under the title *Aussaattage*
English edition published by Floris Books

British Library CIP Data available
ISBN 978-178250-733-8
ISSN: 2052-5761
Printed in Poland through Hussar

 Floris Books supports sustainable forest management by printing this book on materials made from wood that comes from responsible sources and reclaimed material

MIX
Paper from
responsible sources
FSC® C167221

Contents

Preface

Just after last year's calendar was printed, we heard that Matthias Thun unexpectedly passed away. A few months before I had visited Matthias and his children, Titia and Friedrich, as I often did. We had discussed a closer working together. We also looked through some rough layout drafts I brought of the English version you now have, and talked about how to make the calendar more easily understood by those who had little previous experience of using it.

Some things, like the tree sowing and cutting times, were only given as dates in the German calendar. But in English our readers are spread from New Zealand to Alaska, so we needed more precise times that could be used in time zones far in the east or west. Together we calculated the times that first appeared last year in the English edition.

After seeking and listening to feedback from our readers, we have completely redesigned this year's calendar, mainly to give more space to practical hints of what to do in the garden or on the farm each month. The introductory and background text has been rewritten to help readers understand the principles behind the calendar.

We hope that this helps and would be happy to hear suggestions from our readers.

Christian Maclean
Editor, Floris Books

What are the basic principles of the calendar?

The information in this guide is based on over sixty years of research by Maria Thun, who lived in central Germany and for over fifty years produced this annual calendar. After her death in 2012 her son Matthias continued the work, and it is now produced by her grandchildren, Titia and Friedrich.

The principle that underlies this guide is that the Moon has a significant influence over the Earth. Not only does it control the tides, but it influences all living organisms, including the way plants grow.

From our perspective on Earth, the Sun passes through twelve star constellations every year – the signs of the zodiac, from Aries to Pisces. The Moon also passes through these constellations, but because the Moon circles the Earth once a month, it passes through all twelve constellations about once every month.

Each constellation is associated with one of the four classical elements – earth, water, air or fire. And each of these elements affects a different part of a plant:

- the earth element affects the roots
- the water element affects the leaves
- the air element affects the flowers
- and the fire element affects the fruit and seed

It is easy to understand why: the roots are down in the earth, the leaves are full of water, the flowers' perfume is carried by the air, and fire (or warmth) is essential for fruit to ripen.

Through the course of many agricultural trials over several decades, Maria Thun showed that plants thrived, yields were increased, and harvested produce lasted longer if plants were tended at specific times, according to the part of the plant that the grower wanted to enhance. For example, carrots thrived if they were tended during root times, and apples thrived if they were tended during fruit times. This calendar gives you all the information you need to tend your plants at the best possible times, for the best possible outcomes.

The details of this calendar take into account all aspects of lunar and solar cycles, star constellations and the movement of planets. It is used every year by people all over the world to decide when to sow, plant and harvest fruit (including grapes for making biodynamic wine), vegetables, flowers and crops, as well as by beekeepers and people who make butter and cheese, since all of these are influenced by the movement of the Moon.

How do I use the calendar?

Different parts of a plant are cultivated for food or other uses. Plants can therefore be divided into four groups:

- Root plants, like carrots and potatoes
- Leaf plants like lettuce, spinach and the cabbage family, as well as herbs
- Flower plants, like broccoli and cauliflower, as well as ornamental flowers
- Fruit plants, like beans and tomatoes, as well as the obvious apples, oranges, grapes, and so on

There is a full list of types of plants on p. 66 so you can be confident about which type of plant you're growing.

The growth of all garden and farm plants and crops is enhanced when the plants are sown, transplanted, hoed, weeded, cut back and even harvested when the Moon is in a constellation that matches the plant type.

The twelve constellations are grouped into four different types, which correspond to the four types of time in this guide:

- Virgo (♍), Capricorn (♑), Taurus (♉)   Root
- Libra (♎), Aquarius (♒), Gemini (♊)   Flower
- Scorpio (♏), Pisces (♓), Cancer (♋)   Leaf
- Sagittarius (♐), Aries (♈), Leo (♌)   Fruit, seed

What's shown in the calendar?

The dates are listed down the left-hand column.

The hours are listed along the top, from 0 (midnight) to 12 (noon) and on to 24 (midnight again).

Transplanting Time (see p. 11)

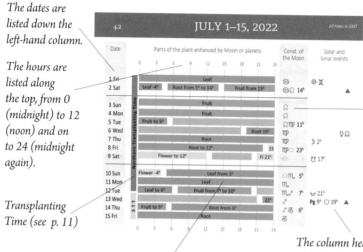

The column headed Const. of the Moon shows which star constellation the Moon is passing through, on that day.

The column headed Solar and lunar events shows other information about the Moon, Sun and sometimes other astronomical events (you'll find more about that in 'I'd like to understand the astronomy in more detail' p. 10).

The horizontal coloured bars show the hours that are optimal for working on which type of plants. There are four types of time: Root (brown bar), Flower (yellow bar), Leaf (green bar) and Fruit (red bar). There are also grey bars which are unfavourable times for working on any crop. (To find out why, skip ahead to 'Why are other astronomical events important' p. 12.)

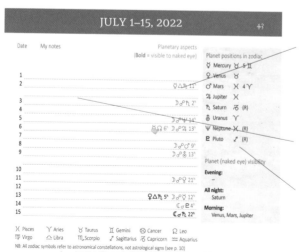

Planetary aspects and other astronomical information (see 'Why are other astronomical events important' p.12) are indicated on the right.

There is space for your own notes here.

The final (tinted) column shows which constellation the planets are in, and purely for those interested in astronomy, the naked-eye visibility of the planets (see 'Planets' p. 14).

Times and symbols

What time zone is the calendar in?

The times shown in this calendar are GMT. In the UK and Ireland remember to add an hour to all the times during British Summer Time.

If you are not in the UK, you'll need to add or subtract from the times in the charts according to your location (see page 17 'Converting to local times'). If you download the companion Biodynamic Gardening Calendar app, which uses data from this calendar and allows you to look up planting information while you're on the go, the app adjusts the times automatically to your location, but does not give as much detail as the printed calendar. (Details of the app are on the inside back cover).

Note that Fruit, Flower, Root and Leaf times normally don't last for precisely one day. The Moon moves in and out of different constellations at different times, so a Flower time might start at 11 am on a Monday and finish at 5 pm on a Wednesday. Use the coloured bars to pinpoint whether conditions are favourable at a particular time on a particular day.

Do I need to understand all the symbols?

You do not need to understand all the astronomical background to grow better vegetables! If it is too daunting, just ignore it, and follow the practical hints for the type of plant you are growing at the times shown by the horizontal coloured bars.

Why does the calendar recommend certain activities in the middle of the night?

Don't worry, no midnight planting is required! The calendar works for gardeners and farmers around the world, and one person's midnight is another person's morning or early evening. Just choose the times that work best for you. There are usually plenty of options for tending each type of plant.

Why does the calendar recommend that I harvest and store leaf plants during a Fruit and Flower times?

It may seem counter-intuitive, but it has been shown that Fruit and Flower times are best for harvesting and storing leaf plants such as lettuce, spinach and herbs.

I'd like to understand the astronomy in more detail
Star signs and constellations

The **zodiac** is a group of twelve constellations of stars, which the Sun, Moon and all the planets pass on their circuits as seen from the Earth. We know them as the zodiac – Scorpio, Cancer, Aries, etc. – but in the context of this guide, these names are used to indicate the visible star *constellations* rather than the astrological *signs* used in horoscopes. (For those who are into astronomy and astrology, the difference is that they are out of sync, as shown in the diagram below.)

The Moon takes about 27½ days to orbit the Earth, passing through all twelve constellations in that time. This rhythm is called the *sidereal month.*

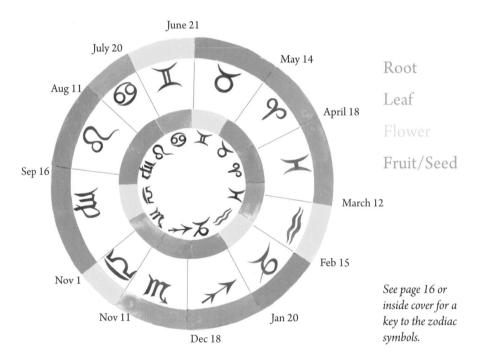

Root

Leaf

Flower

Fruit/Seed

See page 16 or inside cover for a key to the zodiac symbols.

*The outer circle shows the varying sizes of the visible **constellations** of the zodiac. The dates on this outer circle are the approximate dates on which the Sun enters the constellation (from year to year the actual date can change by one day because of leap years). The inner circle shows the divisions into equal sections of 30° corresponding to the **signs** used in astrology.*

Transplanting Time and ascending or descending Moon

From midwinter through to midsummer the Sun rises earlier and sets later each day, and its path across the sky ascends higher and higher. From midsummer until midwinter this is reversed: the days get shorter and the midday Sun shines from an ever-lower point in the sky. This annual ascending and descending of the Sun creates our seasons. In the northern hemisphere the winter solstice occurs in December when the Sun is in the constellation of Sagittarius, and the summer solstice occurs in June when the Sun is in Gemini. At any point from Sagittarius to Gemini, the Sun is ascending, while from Gemini to Sagittarius, it is descending. In the southern hemisphere, this is reversed.

The Moon (and all the planets) follow approximately the same path as the Sun around the zodiac but instead of taking a year, the Moon takes only about 27½ days to complete one cycle. This means that the Moon will ascend for about fourteen days, and then descend for about fourteen days.

When the Moon is *ascending,* plant sap rises more strongly. The upper part of the plant fills with sap and vitality. This is therefore a good time for cutting scions (young shoots for grafting). Fruit harvested during this period remains fresh for longer when stored.

When the Moon is *descending,* plants take root more readily and connect well with their new location. This period is referred to as the **Transplanting Time**, even though the period is actually optimal for a range of growing activities. Transplanting is when plants are moved from one location to another, for example when young plants are moved from the seedbed into their final growing position, but also when the gardener wishes to strengthen the root development of young fruit trees, shrubs or pot plants by frequently re-potting them. Note that sowing is the moment when a seed is put into the soil, and this can

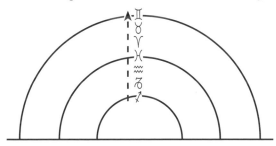

The northern hemisphere ascending Moon, showing the Moon's arc across the sky getting higher and higher for about 14 days, with the Moon moving from Sagittarius to Gemini.

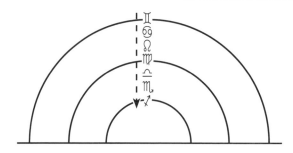

*The northern hemisphere descending Moon (**Transplanting Time**), showing the Moon's arc across the sky getting lower and lower for about 14 days, with the Moon moving from Gemini to Sagittarius.*

be done during either the ascending or descending period. We use the term 'transplanting' rather than just 'planting' to avoid confusion with sowing.

Additionally, because sap movement is slower during the descending Moon, it is a good time for trimming hedges, pruning trees and felling timber as well as applying compost to meadows, pastures and orchards.

You will sometimes see a reference to **Northern Transplanting Times** and Southern Transplanting Times. These are just a quick way to refer to the period of the descending Moon in either hemisphere.

In the 'Solar and lunar events' panel the date and time of highest Moon ($\cap$) is shown, after which the Moon descends, likewise lowest Moon ($\cup$) after which the Moon ascends. For the southern hemisphere these are the opposite way round: what is shown as highest Moon is the lowest Moon there.

One final note on the ascending and descending Moon: it is important to distinguish the journey of the Moon through the zodiac (sidereal rhythm) from the phases (waxing and waning); in any given constellation there may be a waxing or waning Moon.

Why are other astronomical events important?

There are many astronomical events in our skies, which also have an effect on the Earth, and this section gives more details about them and their effects.

They are important because some of them have an unfavourable effect on plant growth for some hours, and you shouldn't do any work in the garden during these times. These so-called *unfavourable times* are shown in the calendar as grey horizontal bars.

If you are not interested in astronomy, you can simply skip this section, but avoid doing anything in the garden during the times marked as unfavourable.

More Moon rhythms
The phases

The calendar pages show the phases of the Moon under 'Solar and lunar events'.

● New Moon   ☽ Waxing half Moon (first quarter)
○ Full Moon   ☾ Waning half Moon (last quarter)

This rhythm also takes about one month. Called the *synodic month,* it is a little longer – about 29½ days – than the sidereal rhythm that relates to movement through the constellations of the zodiac. This cycle does not have much effect on plant growth, and we take no account of it in this calendar; they are merely shown for those people who want to have a complete picture of the Moon's rhythms.

The Moon's nodes

The Moon's path through the zodiac is not exactly the same as the Sun's path (which is called the ecliptic). Seen from the Earth, the Moon's path is inclined by about 5° to the ecliptic. Twice a month, the Moon crosses the ecliptic, the Sun's path. These crossing points are called nodes. One crosses from below the ecliptic to above it and this is called the ascending node (shown as ☊ in the calendar under 'Solar and lunar events'). About two weeks later, it crosses from above to below; this is the descending node (shown as ☋). The times around the nodes are shown as unfavourable times (grey bars in the calendar). Both ascending and descending nodes have a negative effect on plant growth.

Eclipses

If a New Moon occurs at a node there is a solar eclipse, as the Moon is directly in front of the Sun. If a Full Moon occurs at a node there is a lunar eclipse, where the Earth's shadow falls on the Moon. Even if the eclipse is not visible from where you are, it has an unfavourable effect on plant growth and is shown as an unfavourable time in the calendar (grey bars).

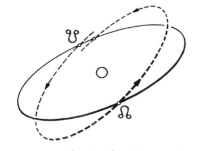

The Sun's path (solid line) and the Moon's path (dashed line) seen from the Earth (centre). The angle is exaggerated for clarity. The descending node (crossing point) is behind, and ascending node in front. (Note that the following node will not be in the same position: the nodes move.)

Apogee and perigee

The Moon travels on an almost circular ellipse around the Earth. This means that sometimes the Moon is a little closer to the Earth, and sometimes a little further away. The point at which the Moon is closest to the Earth is called perigee (shown as **Pg** under 'Solar and lunar events'). Conversely, the point at which the Moon is furthest from the Earth is called apogee (shown as **Ag**).

Perigee (**Pg**) is an unfavourable time (grey bars) for gardening work.

However, around apogee (**Ag**) the Moon stimulates flowering and fruiting. The calendar bars take account of this effect, which can mean that they diverge from the underlying Moon/constellation effect.

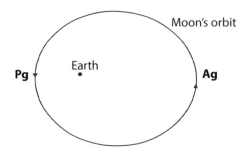

The elliptical orbit of the Moon around the Earth (exaggerated), showing closest (Perigee) and furthest (Apogee) positions.

The Sun and the zodiac

The Sun's movement through the zodiac takes a year and determines the seasons on Earth. The constellation through which the Sun is passing is always shown on the first entry of a calendar page, and if it changes during the month that is shown on the appropriate day. Remember that the calendar shows the visible astronomical constellations, and not the astrological signs, so the dates are out of sync! (See p. 10.)

Some activities depend on which constellation the Sun is in (for instance, making biodynamic preparations).

Planets

The planets, too, have an effect on plant growth. The far-right panel on the calendar pages shows which constellation each planet is passing. The planets mostly move in direct motion – that is, in the same direction as the Sun and Moon – but unlike the Moon, for some time they move in the opposite direction, which is called retrograde motion. (Retrograde motion can strengthen the effect of the planet.) This time is shown as R, with the date indicating when the retrograde motion begins. When the planet begins to move in direct motion again, it is shown as D.

The visibility of the planets to the naked eye is shown below this panel. This is purely an aid to personal observation and has no effect at all on farming or gardening! Note that the furthest planets, Neptune, Uranus and Pluto, cannot be seen with the naked eye.

Aspects

Aspects are particular angular relationships of planets, the Sun and the Moon (collectively called *celestial bodies*), as seen from the Earth. The main ones are *conjunctions*, which is when two celestial bodies pass each other; *oppositions*, which is when they are opposite each other; and *trines*, which is when they are 120° apart.

σ conjunction   ♂° opposition   △ (or ▲) trine

For those interested in observing the planets, the aspects visible to the naked eye are shown in bold type.

Conjunctions

Conjunctions (shown as σ) occur when two planets stand behind one another in space. Usually only the planet closest to the Earth has any influence on plant growth. If this influence is stronger than that of the Moon, cosmic disturbances can occur that irritate the plants and cause problems with growth.

This negative effect is increased if the Moon or Sun stand directly in front of a planet – called an *occultation* (●). In the case of Sun and Moon, this is called an eclipse. Sowing at these times will harm future growth and damage a plant's ability to reproduce. These times are marked as an unfavourable time (grey bar).

Oppositions

An opposition (shown as ♂°) occurs if two celestial bodies are opposite one another – 180° apart. You cannot see both planets during an opposition because one will be above the horizon, the other below. Their rays fall on to the Earth and positively stimulate the seeds sown at that moment. In trials, Maria Thun found that seedlings transplanted at times of opposition resulted in a slightly higher yield. While the opposition is shown under the planetary aspects, it is not otherwise noted on the calendar pages.

Trines

Trines (shown as △) occur when planets are 120° from one another. The two planets are usually both standing in the same type of constellation – Aries and Leo for example are both Fruit (fire or warmth) constellations. Generally, the positive effect of the trine overrules the underlying lunar constellation. There may therefore be a Fruit time shown in the calendar despite the Moon being in a Leaf (or other) constellation. To show that this is deliberate, there is a coloured ▲ under 'Solar and lunar events'.

Sometimes when two planets are in a trine, they are in different types of constellations. The trine is shown as △ under planetary aspects on the right-hand page, but these trines have no effect on plant growth and are not shown as coloured ▲ under 'Solar and lunar events' on the left page.

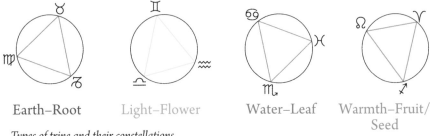

| Earth–Root | Light–Flower | Water–Leaf | Warmth–Fruit/Seed |

Types of trine and their constellations

Astronomical symbols

Constellations		*Planets*		*Aspects*	
♓	Pisces	☉	Sun	☊	Ascending node
♈	Aries	☽	Moon (first qtr)	☋	Descending node
♉	Taurus	☾	Moon (last qtr)	⌢	Highest Moon
♊	Gemini	☿	Mercury	⌣	Lowest Moon
♋	Cancer	♀	Venus	**Pg**	Perigee
♌	Leo	♂	Mars	**Ag**	Apogee
♍	Virgo	♃	Jupiter	☍	Opposition
♎	Libra	♄	Saturn	☌	Conjunction
♏	Scorpio	♅	Uranus	☉	Eclipse/occultation
♐	Sagittarius	♆	Neptune	☾	Lunar eclipse
♑	Capricorn	♇	Pluto	△	Trine (or ▲)
♒	Aquarius	○	Full Moon	D	Direct motion
		●	New Moon	R	Retrograde motion

Converting to local time

Times given are Greenwich Mean Time (GMT), using the 24-hour clock with ^{h} after the time. Thus 15^h is 3 pm. **No account is taken of daylight saving (summer) time (DST).** Note 0^h is midnight at the beginning of a date, and 24^h is midnight at the end of the date.

Add (+) or subtract (−) times as below. For countries not listed check local time against GMT.

Europe

Britain, Ireland, Portugal: GMT
  (DST March 27 to Oct 29, $+1^h$)
Iceland: GMT (no DST)
Central Europe: $+1^h$
  (DST March 27 to Oct 29, $+2^h$)
Eastern Europe (Finland etc.): $+2^h$
  (DST March 27 to Oct 29, $+3^h$)
Russia (Moscow): $+3^h$ (no DST)
Georgia: $+4^h$ (no DST)

Africa/Asia

South Africa, Namibia: $+2^h$ (no DST)
Kenya: $+3^h$ (no DST)
Egypt: $+2^h$ (no DST)
Israel: $+2^h$ (DST March 25 to
  Oct 29, $+3^h$)
India: $+5\frac{1}{2}^h$ (no DST)
Philippines, China: $+8^h$ (no DST)
Japan, Korea: $+9^h$ (no DST)

Australia/New Zealand

Western Australia: $+8^h$ (no DST)
Northern Territory: $+9\frac{1}{2}^h$ (no DST)
South Australia: $+9\frac{1}{2}^h$ (DST to April
  2 and from Oct 2, $+10\frac{1}{2}^h$)

Queensland: $+10^h$ (no DST)
ACT, NSW, Victoria, Tasmania: $+10^h$
  (DST to April 2 & from Oct 2, $+11^h$)
New Zealand: $+12^h$ (DST to April 2
  and from Sep 25, $+13^h$)

North America

Newfoundland Standard Time: $-3\frac{1}{2}^h$
  (DST March 13 to Nov 5, $-2\frac{1}{2}^h$)
Atlantic Standard Time: -4^h
  (DST March 13 to Nov 5, -3^h)
Eastern Standard Time: -5^h
  (DST March 13 to Nov 5, -4^h)
Central Standard Time: -6^h
  (DST March 13 to Nov 5, -5^h,
  except Saskatchewan with no
  DST)
Mountain Standard Time: -7^h (DST
  March 13 to Nov 5, -6^h, except AZ
  with no DST)
Pacific Standard Time: -8^h
  (DST March 13 to Nov 5, -7^h)
Alaska Standard Time: -9^h
  (DST March 13 to Nov 5, -8^h)
Hawaii Standard Time: -10^h (no
  DST)
Mexico (mostly CST): -6^h
  (DST April 3 to Oct 29, -5^h)

South America

Argentina: -3^h (no DST)
Brazil (Brasilia): -3^h (no DST)
Chile: -4^h (DST to April 2 and from
  Sep 4, -3^h)
Columbia, Peru: -5^h (no DST)

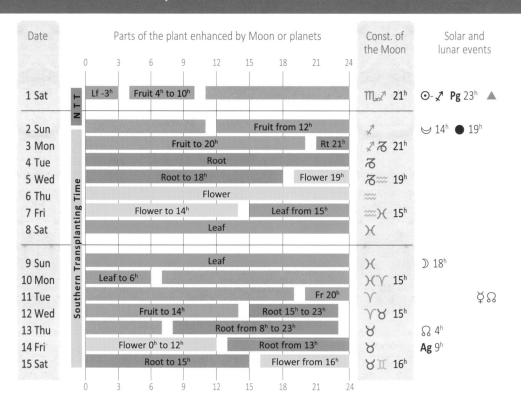

Date	Parts of the plant enhanced by Moon or planets	Const. of the Moon	Solar and lunar events
1 Sat	NTT / Lf -3ʰ / Fruit 4ʰ to 10ʰ	♏♐ 21ʰ	☉-♐ **Pg** 23ʰ ▲
2 Sun	Fruit from 12ʰ	♐	☋ 14ʰ ● 19ʰ
3 Mon	Fruit to 20ʰ / Rt 21ʰ	♐♑ 21ʰ	
4 Tue	Root	♑	
5 Wed	Root to 18ʰ / Flower 19ʰ	♑♒ 19ʰ	
6 Thu	Flower	♒	
7 Fri	Flower to 14ʰ / Leaf from 15ʰ	♒♓ 15ʰ	
8 Sat	Leaf	♓	
9 Sun	Leaf	♓	☽ 18ʰ
10 Mon	Leaf to 6ʰ	♓♈ 15ʰ	
11 Tue	Fr 20ʰ	♈	☿ ♌
12 Wed	Fruit to 14ʰ / Root 15ʰ to 23ʰ	♈♉ 15ʰ	
13 Thu	Root from 8ʰ to 23ʰ	♉	♌ 4ʰ
14 Fri	Flower 0ʰ to 12ʰ / Root from 13ʰ	♉	**Ag** 9ʰ
15 Sat	Root to 15ʰ / Flower from 16ʰ	♉♊ 16ʰ	

Southern Transplanting Time (shown along left side, rows 2 Sun–15 Sat)

Transplanting Time
(time of descending Moon in northern hemisphere)
Dec 20 to Jan 2 12ʰ and Jan 16 12ʰ to Jan 29 21ʰ

Fruit times

- Tend fruit plants (beans, grains, tomatoes) during these times.
- Plant bare-root fruit trees and soft fruit shrubs on unfrozen soil.

Leaf times

- Tend leafy plants (like lettuce) during these times.
- Sow winter lettuce and leeks in a greenhouse, or in warm regions in pots.

Flower times

- Tend flowering plants (broccoli, roses) during these times.
- Sow cauliflower in warm regions in pots.
- Plant flowering shurbs.

Root times

- Tend root plants (carrots, potatoes) during these times.
- Sow turnips in a greenhouse.

Date	My notes	Planetary aspects (**Bold** = visible to naked eye)
1		☉△♁ 10ʰ
2		
3		☽☌♀ 10ʰ ☽☌♇ 16ʰ
4		☽☌☿ 3ʰ ☽☌♄ 19ʰ
5		
6		☽☌♃ 3ʰ
7		☽☌♆ 13ʰ
8		
9		☉☌♀ 1ʰ
10		
11		☿☊ 7ʰ ☽☌♁ 12ʰ
12		
13		
14		
15		☽☍♂ 2ʰ

Planet positions in zodiac

☿ Mercury ♐ 1 ♑ (14 R)
♀ Venus ♐ (R)
♂ Mars ♏
♃ Jupiter ♒
♄ Saturn ♑
♁ Uranus ♈ (R)
♆ Neptune ♒
♇ Pluto ♐

Planet (naked eye) visibility

Evening:
Venus (to Jan 6), Jupiter, Saturn

All night: –

Morning:
Venus (from Jan 10), Mars

♓ Pisces	♈ Aries	♉ Taurus	♊ Gemini	♋ Cancer	♌ Leo
♍ Virgo	♎ Libra	♏ Scorpio	♐ Sagittarius	♑ Capricorn	♒ Aquarius

NB: All zodiac symbols refer to astronomical constellations, not astrological signs (see p. 10)

Milk processing

When **milk processing** it is best to avoid unfavourable times. This applies to both butter and cheese making. Milk which has been produced at Fruit times yields the highest butterfat content. This is also the case on days with a tendency for thunderstorms. Times of perigee (**Pg**) are almost always unfavourable for milk processing and even yoghurt will not turn out well. Starter cultures from such days decay rapidly and it is advisable to produce double the amount the day before. Milk loves Flower and Fruit times best of all. Leaf times are unsuitable.

Southern hemisphere

Southern Transplanting Time
Jan 2 16ʰ to Jan 16 8ʰ and Jan 30 1ʰ to Feb 12

Harvest time for seeds (*Avoid unfavourable times*)
- **Fruit seeds:** Jan 2 12ʰ to Jan 3 20ʰ and other Fruit times.
- **Flower seeds:** Jan 5 19ʰ to Jan 7 14ʰ and other Flower times.
- **Leaf seeds:** Jan 7 15ʰ to Jan 10 6ʰ and other Leaf times.
- **Root seeds:** Jan 3 21ʰ to Jan 5 18ʰ and other Root times.

Date	Parts of the plant enhanced by Moon or planets	Const. of the Moon	Solar and lunar events
16 Sun	Flower	♊	☉-♐ ♑ 10ʰ
17 Mon	Flower to 23ʰ	♊	○ 24ʰ
18 Tue	Leaf from 0ʰ	♋ 0ʰ	☉-♑
19 Wed	Leaf to 16ʰ / Fruit from 17ʰ	♋♌ 17ʰ	
20 Thu	Fruit	♌	
21 Fri	Fruit	♌	
22 Sat	Fruit to 10ʰ / Root from 11ʰ	♌♍ 11ʰ	
23 Sun	Root	♍	
24 Mon	Root	♍	
25 Tue	Root to 20ʰ / Fl 21ʰ	♍♎ 21ʰ	☾ 14ʰ
26 Wed	Flower	♎	
27 Thu	1ʰ / Leaf from 10ʰ	♎♏ 4ʰ	☊ 6ʰ
28 Fri	Leaf	♏	
29 Sat	Leaf to 6ʰ / Fruit from 7ʰ	♏♐ 7ʰ	☋ 23ʰ
30 Sun	Fruit to 18ʰ	♐	Pg 7ʰ
31 Mon	Root 20ʰ	♐♑ 8ʰ	

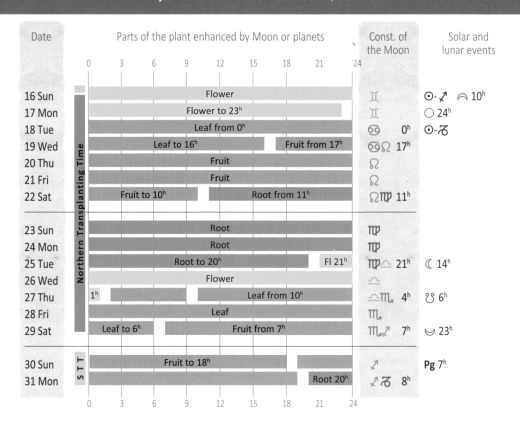

Northern Transplanting Time

STT

Transplanting Time
(time of descending Moon in northern hemisphere)
Jan 16 12ʰ to Jan 29 21ʰ

Leaf times
- Tend leafy plants (like lettuce) during these times.
- Sow lettuce and cabbage in greenhouse.

Root times
- Tend root plants (carrots, potatoes) during these times.
- In mild regions plant garlic.

Fruit times
- Tend fruit plants (beans, grains, tomatoes) during these times.
- The Transplanting Time is a good time for pruning **fruit trees, vines and hedges.** Fruit and Flower times are preferred for this work. Avoid unfavourable times.
- In mild regions sow aubergines (eggplant) and chili peppers.

Flower times
- Tend flowering plants (broccoli, roses) during these times.
- Prune **vines, fruit trees and hedges** – see Fruit times above.
- In mild regions (or a greenhouse) sow begonias and cannas.

Date	My notes	Planetary aspects

(Bold = visible to naked eye)

16		$\odot\,_\sigma\,\text{P}\,15^h$ $\;\;\;\mathcal{D}\,_{\sigma^o}\,\text{♀}\,21^h$
17		$\mathcal{D}\,_{\sigma^o}\,\text{P}\,21^h$
18		$\mathbb{C}\,_{\sigma^o}\,\text{☿}\,21^h$
19		$\mathbb{C}\,_{\sigma^o}\,\hbar\,13^h$
20		$\mathbb{C}\,_{\sigma^o}\,\text{♃}\,23^h$
21		
22		$\mathbb{C}\,_{\sigma^o}\,\text{♆}\,6^h$
23		$\odot\,_\sigma\,\text{☿}\,10^h$
24		
25		$\mathbb{C}\,_{\sigma^o}\,\text{⛢}\,23^h$
26		
27		
28		
29		$\text{☿}\,_\sigma\,\text{P}\,4^h$ $\;\;\mathbb{C}\,_\sigma\,\text{♂}\,15^h$
30		$\mathbb{C}\,_\sigma\,\text{♀}\,3^h$
31		$\mathbb{C}\,_\sigma\,\text{☿}\,2^h$ $\;\;\mathbb{C}\,_\sigma\,\text{P}\,5^h$

Planet positions in zodiac

☿	Mercury	♑ 27 ♐	(R)
♀	Venus	♐	(R 29 D)
♂	Mars	♏ 22 ♐	
♃	Jupiter	♒	
♄	Saturn	♑	
⛢	Uranus	♈	(R 18 D)
♆	Neptune	♒	
P	Pluto	♐	

Planet (naked eye) visibility

Evening:
Jupiter, Saturn (to Jan 21)

All night:
–

Morning:
Venus, Mars

♓ Pisces	♈ Aries	♉ Taurus	♊ Gemini
♋ Cancer	♌ Leo		
♍ Virgo	♎ Libra	♏ Scorpio	♐ Sagittarius
♑ Capricorn	♒ Aquarius		

My notes

Southern hemisphere

Southern Transplanting Time
Jan 2 to Jan 16 8^h and Jan 30 1^h to Feb 12

Harvest time for seeds (*Avoid unfavourable times*)
- **Fruit seeds:** Jan 19 17^h to Jan 22 10^h and other Fruit times.
- **Flower seeds:** Jan 18 0^h to Jan 19 16^h and other Flower times.
- **Leaf seeds:** Jan 27 10^h to Jan 29 6^h and other Leaf times.
- **Root seeds:** Jan 22 11^h to Jan 25 20^h and other Root times.

Control slugs from Jan 18 0^h to Jan 19 16^h.

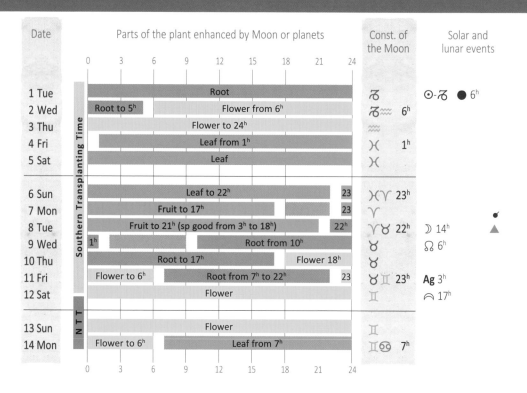

Date	Parts of the plant enhanced by Moon or planets	Const. of the Moon	Solar and lunar events
1 Tue	Root	♑	☉-♑ ● 6ʰ
2 Wed	Root to 5ʰ / Flower from 6ʰ	♑♒ 6ʰ	
3 Thu	Flower to 24ʰ	♒	
4 Fri	Leaf from 1ʰ	♓ 1ʰ	
5 Sat	Leaf	♓	
6 Sun	Leaf to 22ʰ · 23	♓♈ 23ʰ	
7 Mon	Fruit to 17ʰ · 23	♈	
8 Tue	Fruit to 21ʰ (sp good from 3ʰ to 18ʰ) · 22	♈♉ 22ʰ	☽ 14ʰ
9 Wed	1ʰ · Root from 10ʰ	♉ · ☊ 6ʰ	
10 Thu	Root to 17ʰ / Flower 18ʰ	♉	
11 Fri	Flower to 6ʰ / Root from 7ʰ to 22ʰ · 23	♉♊ 23ʰ	**Ag** 3ʰ
12 Sat	Flower	♊	⌒ 17ʰ
13 Sun	Flower	♊	
14 Mon	Flower to 6ʰ / Leaf from 7ʰ	♊♋ 7ʰ	

Southern Transplanting Time · NTT

Transplanting Time
(time of descending Moon in northern hemisphere)
Feb 12 19ʰ to Feb 26 5ʰ

Leaf times
- Tend leafy plants (like lettuce) during these times.
- Transplant lettuce and cabbage during Transplanting Time.

Root times
- Tend root plants (carrots, potatoes) during these times.

Fruit times
- Tend fruit plants (beans, grains, tomatoes) during these times.
- **Vines, fruit trees and shrubs** can be pruned during Transplanting Time from Feb 12 19ʰ selecting Flower and Fruit times as preference. Avoid unfavourable times.

Flower times
- Tend flowering plants (broccoli, roses) during these times.
- Prune **vines, fruit trees and shrubs** – see Fruit times above.
- Take **willow cuttings for hedges and fences** *outside* Transplanting Time (to Feb 12 15ʰ). In warm areas *during* Transplanting Time to avoid too strong a sap current.

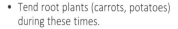

Date	My notes	Planetary aspects
		(**Bold** = visible to naked eye)

Date	Planetary aspects
1	☽ ☌ ♄ 11^h
2	
3	☽ ☌ ♃ 0^h
4	☽ ☌ ♆ 0^h ☉ ☌ ♄ 19^h
5	
6	
7	☽ ● ♅ 20^h
8	♂ △ ♅ 15^h
9	
10	
11	☿ ☌ ♇ 14^h
12	
13	☽ ☍ ♂ 4^h ☽ ☍ ♀ 6^h
14	☽ ☍ ♇ 6^h ☽ ☍ ☿ 10^h

Planet positions in zodiac

☿	Mercury	♐	13 ♑
			(R 4 D)
♀	Venus	♐	
♂	Mars	♐	
♃	Jupiter	♒	
♄	Saturn	♑	
♅	Uranus	♈	
♆	Neptune	♒ 8 ♓	
♇	Pluto	♐	

Planet (naked eye) visibility

Evening:
Jupiter

All night: –

Morning:
Mercury (from Feb 2), Venus, Mars

♓ Pisces	♈ Aries	♉ Taurus	♊ Gemini	♋ Cancer	♌ Leo
♍ Virgo	♎ Libra	♏ Scorpio	♐ Sagittarius	♑ Capricorn	♒ Aquarius

NB: All zodiac symbols refer to astronomical constellations, not astrological signs (see p. 10)

My notes

Southern hemisphere

Southern Transplanting Time
Jan 30 to Feb 12 15^h and Feb 26 9^h to March 11

Harvest time for seeds (*Avoid unfavourable times*)
- **Fruit seeds:** Feb 6 23^h to Feb 8 21^h and other Fruit times.
- **Flower seeds:** Feb 2 6^h to Feb 3 24^h and Feb 11 23^h to Feb 14 6^h.
- **Leaf seeds:** Feb 4 1^h to Feb 6 22^h and other Leaf times.
- **Root seeds:** Jan 31 20^h to Feb 2 5^h and other Root times.

Control slugs from Feb 14 7^h to Feb 15 23^h.

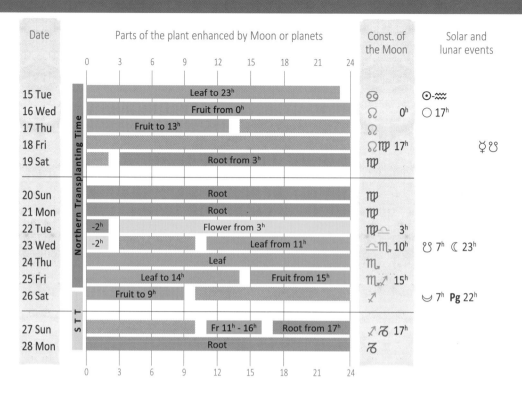

Date	Parts of the plant enhanced by Moon or planets	Const. of the Moon	Solar and lunar events
15 Tue	Leaf to 23^h	♋	☉-♒
16 Wed	Fruit from 0^h	♌ 0^h	○ 17^h
17 Thu	Fruit to 13^h	♌	
18 Fri		♌♍ 17^h	☿ ♂
19 Sat	Root from 3^h	♍	
20 Sun	Root	♍	
21 Mon	Root	♍	
22 Tue	−2^h Flower from 3^h	♍♎ 3^h	
23 Wed	−2^h Leaf from 11^h	♎♏ 10^h	♂ 7^h ☾ 23^h
24 Thu	Leaf	♏	
25 Fri	Leaf to 14^h Fruit from 15^h	♏♐ 15^h	
26 Sat	Fruit to 9^h	♐	☋ 7^h **Pg** 22^h
27 Sun	Fr 11^h – 16^h Root from 17^h	♐♑ 17^h	
28 Mon	Root	♑	

Northern Transplanting Time

STT

Date	My notes	Planetary aspects (**Bold** = visible to naked eye)

Date		Planetary aspects
15		$\mathbb{D} \, \sigma^{\circ} \, \hbar \; 21^h$
16		$\mathbf{Q \, \sigma \, \sigma^{\!\!\!\nearrow} \; 14^h}$
17		$\mathbb{C} \, \sigma^{\circ} \, 2\!\!\!\downarrow \; 17^h$
18		$\mathbb{C} \, \sigma^{\circ} \, \Psi \; 13^h \;\; \breve{\varphi} \, \vartheta \; 14^h$
19		
20		
21		
22		$\mathbb{C} \, \sigma^{\circ} \, \hat{\delta} \; 5^h$
23		
24		
25		
26		
27		$\mathbb{C} \, \sigma \, \mathbf{Q} \; 9^h \;\; \mathbb{C} \, \sigma \, \sigma^{\!\!\!\nearrow} \; 10^h \;\; \mathbb{C} \, \sigma \, \mathbf{P} \; 15^h$
28		$\mathbb{C} \, \sigma \, \breve{\varphi} \; 22^h$

Planet positions in zodiac

$\breve{\varphi}$	Mercury	♑
♀	Venus	♐
♂	Mars	♐
♃	Jupiter	♒
♄	Saturn	♑
♅	Uranus	♈
♆	Neptune	♓
♇	Pluto	♐

Planet (naked eye) visibility

Evening:
    Jupiter (to Feb 21)

All night: –

Morning:
    Mercury (to Feb 25), Venus, Mars

♓ Pisces	♈ Aries	♉ Taurus	♊ Gemini	♋ Cancer	♌ Leo
♍ Virgo	♎ Libra	♏ Scorpio	♐ Sagittarius	♑ Capricorn	♒ Aquarius

NB: All zodiac symbols refer to astronomical constellations, not astrological signs (see p. 10)

Beekeeping

Remove anti-bird nets and mouse guards to enable clearing flights.

My notes

Southern hemisphere

Southern Transplanting Time
Feb 26 9^h to March 11

Harvest time for seeds (*Avoid unfavourable times*)
- **Fruit seeds:** Feb 16 0^h to Feb 17 13^h and other Fruit times.
- **Flower seeds:** Feb 22 3^h to Feb 23 2^h and other Flower times.
- **Leaf seeds:** Feb 14 7^h to Feb 15 23^h and Feb 23 11^h to Feb 25 14^h.
- **Root seeds:** Feb 19 3^h to Feb 22 2^h and other Root times.

Control slugs from Feb 14 7^h to Feb 15 23^h.

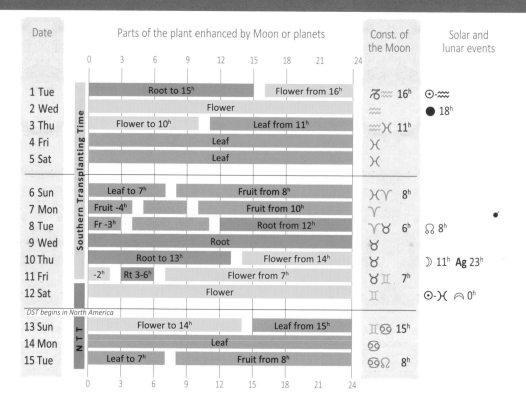

Date	Parts of the plant enhanced by Moon or planets	Const. of the Moon	Solar and lunar events
1 Tue	Root to 15ʰ / Flower from 16ʰ	♑♒ 16ʰ	☉-♒
2 Wed	Flower	♒	● 18ʰ
3 Thu	Flower to 10ʰ / Leaf from 11ʰ	♒♓ 11ʰ	
4 Fri	Leaf	♓	
5 Sat	Leaf	♓	
6 Sun	Leaf to 7ʰ / Fruit from 8ʰ	♓♈ 8ʰ	
7 Mon	Fruit -4ʰ / Fruit from 10ʰ	♈	
8 Tue	Fr -3ʰ / Root from 12ʰ	♈♉ 6ʰ	☍ 8ʰ
9 Wed	Root	♉	
10 Thu	Root to 13ʰ / Flower from 14ʰ	♉	☽ 11ʰ Ag 23ʰ
11 Fri	-2ʰ Rt 3-6ʰ / Flower from 7ʰ	♉♊ 7ʰ	
12 Sat	Flower	♊	☉-♓ ☌ 0ʰ

DST begins in North America

Transplanting Time (NTT)

13 Sun	Flower to 14ʰ / Leaf from 15ʰ	♊♋ 15ʰ	
14 Mon	Leaf	♋	
15 Tue	Leaf to 7ʰ / Fruit from 8ʰ	♋♌ 8ʰ	

Transplanting Time
(time of descending Moon in northern hemisphere)
March 12 2ʰ to March 25 10ʰ

Leaf times

- Tend leafy plants (like lettuce) during these times.
- Transplant spinach and lettuce.

Root times

- Tend root plants (carrots, potatoes) during these times.
- Sow carrots, radishes and turnips.
- Plant artichokes, horseradish and early potatoes.

Fruit times

- Tend fruit plants (beans, grains, tomatoes) during these times.
- Prune fruit trees and shrubs.
- **Cuttings for grafting:** cut outside Transplanting Time during ascending Moon. For fruit trees and shrubs, March 6 8ʰ to March 8 3ʰ, avoiding unfavourable times.
- In warm areas plant cucumbers and tomatoes in pots.

Flower times

- Tend flowering plants (broccoli, roses) during these times.
- **Cuttings for grafting:** cut outside Transplanting Time during ascending Moon. For flowering shrubs, March 1 16ʰ to March 3 10ʰ and March 11 7ʰ to 22ʰ.

Date	My notes	Planetary aspects (**Bold** = visible to naked eye)

1		☽ ☌ ♄ 2^h
2		☿ ☌ ♄ 17^h ☽ ☌ ♃ 21^h
3		♂ ☌ ♇ 9^h ☽ ☌ ♆ 12^h ♀ ☌ ♇ 18^h
4		
5		☉ ☌ ♃ 14^h
6		♀ ☌ ♂ 7^h
7		☽ ☌ ⛢ 7^h
8		
9		
10		
11		
12		
13		☉ ☌ ♆ 12^h ☽ ☍ ♇ 16^h
14		☽ ☍ ♂ 7^h ☽ ☍ ♀ 10^h
15		☽ ☍ ♄ 11^h

Planet positions in zodiac

☿	Mercury	♑	7 ♒
♀	Venus	♐	14 ♑
♂	Mars	♐	4 ♑
♃	Jupiter	♒	
♄	Saturn	♑	
⛢	Uranus	♈	
♆	Neptune	♓	
♇	Pluto	♐	

Planet (naked eye) visibility

Evening:
 –

All night:
 –

Morning:
 Venus, Mars

♓ Pisces	♈ Aries	♉ Taurus	♊ Gemini	♋ Cancer	♌ Leo
♍ Virgo	♎ Libra	♏ Scorpio	♐ Sagittarius	♑ Capricorn	♒ Aquarius

NB: All zodiac symbols refer to astronomical constellations, not astrological signs (see p. 10)

Control pests
(see p. 74 for details)

Slugs: ash from March 13 15^h to March 15 7^h.

Beekeeping

Willow cuttings for **pollen production** are best cut from March 12 2^h to March 13 14^h; and for **honey flow** from March 15 8^h to March 17 24^h. Avoid unfavourable times.

Biodynamic preparations

Pick dandelions in March or April in the mornings during Flower times. The flowers should not be quite open in the centre. Dry them on paper in the shade, not in bright sunlight. Once dried they can be stored until suitably encased and buried in the ground.

Southern hemisphere

Southern Transplanting Time
Feb 26 to March 11 22^h
and March 25 14^h to April 8

Harvest time for seeds (*Avoid unfavourable times*)
- **Fruit seeds:** March 6 8^h to March 8 3^h and March 15 8^h to March 17 24^h.
- **Flower seeds:** March 1 16^h to March 3 10^h and March 11 7^h to March 13 14^h.
- **Leaf seeds:** March 3 11^h to March 6 7^h and March 13 15^h to March 15 7^h.
- **Root seeds:** March 8 12^h to March 10 13^h and other Root times.

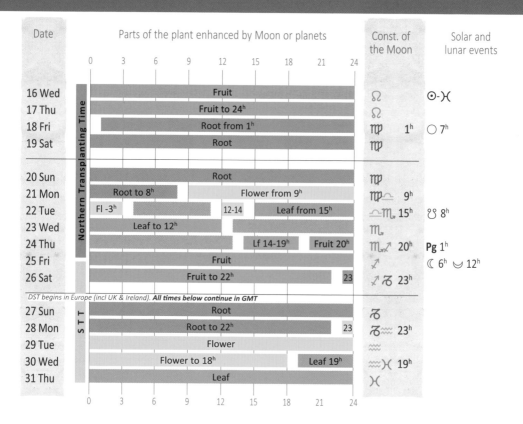

Date	Parts of the plant enhanced by Moon or planets	Const. of the Moon	Solar and lunar events
16 Wed	Fruit	♌	☉-♓
17 Thu	Fruit to 24^h	♌	
18 Fri	Root from 1^h	♍ 1^h	○ 7^h
19 Sat	Root	♍	
20 Sun	Root	♍	
21 Mon	Root to 8^h / Flower from 9^h	♍♎ 9^h	
22 Tue	Fl -3^h / 12-14 / Leaf from 15^h	♎♏ 15^h	☍ 8^h
23 Wed	Leaf to 12^h	♏	
24 Thu	Lf 14-19^h / Fruit 20^h	♏♐ 20^h	**Pg** 1^h
25 Fri	Fruit	♐	☾ 6^h � 12^h
26 Sat	Fruit to 22^h / 23	♐♑ 23^h	
27 Sun	Root	♑	
28 Mon	Root to 22^h / 23	♑♒ 23^h	
29 Tue	Flower	♒	
30 Wed	Flower to 18^h / Leaf 19^h	♒♓ 19^h	
31 Thu	Leaf	♓	

Northern Transplanting Time (vertical label, 16–26)

DST begins in Europe (incl UK & Ireland). All times below continue in GMT

STT (vertical label, 27–28)

Transplanting Time
(time of descending Moon in northern hemisphere)
March 12 to March 25 10^h

Leaf times

- Tend leafy plants (like lettuce) during these times.
- Sow cabbage, Brussels sprouts, endives.

Root times

- Tend root plants during these times.
- Sow parsnips.
- Plant potatoes.

Beekeeping
Cut **willow cuttings** for **honey flow** from March 15 8^h to March 17 24^h. Avoid unfavourable times.

Fruit times

- Tend fruit plants (beans, grains, tomatoes) during these times.
- **Cuttings for grafting:** cut outside Transplanting Time during ascending Moon. For fruit trees and shrubs, March 25 14^h to March 26 22^h, avoiding unfavourable times.
- Sow melon seeds in pots.
- Plant strawberries.

Flower times

- Tend flowering plants (broccoli, roses) during these times.
- **Cuttings for grafting:** cut outside Transplanting Time during ascending Moon. For flowering shrubs, March 28 23^h to March 30 18^h.

+ 1 hour from 27th march.

Date	My notes	Planetary aspects
		(**Bold** = visible to naked eye)

16	
17	☽☌♀ ☿ 2^h ☽☍♃ 14^h ☽☍♆ 23^h
18	
19	
20	
21	☿☌♃ 6^h ☾☍♅ 13^h
22	
23	☿☌♆ 18^h
24	
25	
26	☾☌♇ 22^h
27	
28	☾☌♂ 5^h ☾☌♀ 14^h ☾☌♄ 14^h ♀☌♄ 20^h
29	
30	☾☌♃ 17^h ☾☌♆ 22^h
31	

Planet positions in zodiac

- ☿ Mercury ♒ 22 ♓
- ♀ Venus ♑
- ♂ Mars ♑
- ♃ Jupiter ♒
- ♄ Saturn ♑
- ♅ Uranus ♈
- ♆ Neptune ♓
- ♇ Pluto ♐

Planet (naked eye) visibility

Evening:
–

All night:
–

Morning:
Venus, Mars,
Saturn (from March 22)

♓ Pisces	♈ Aries	♉ Taurus	♊ Gemini	♋ Cancer	♌ Leo
♍ Virgo	♎ Libra	♏ Scorpio	♐ Sagittarius	♑ Capricorn	♒ Aquarius

Biodynamic preparations

Pick dandelions in March or April in the mornings during Flower times. The flowers should not be quite open in the centre. Dry them on paper in the shade, not in bright sunlight. Once dried they can be stored until suitably encased and buried in the ground.

My notes

Southern hemisphere

Southern Transplanting Time
March 25 14^h to April 8

Harvest time for seeds (*Avoid unfavourable times*)
- **Fruit seeds:** March 15 8^h to March 17 24^h and March 24 20^h to March 26 22^h.
- **Flower seeds:** March 21 9^h to March 22 14^h* and March 28 23^h to March 30 18^h.
- **Leaf seeds:** March 22 15^h to March 24 19^h* and March 30 19^h to April 2 16^h.
- **Root seeds:** March 18 1^h to March 21 8^h and March 26 23^h to March 28 22^h.

Tip

Not sure what type of plant your vegetable is?
- See Crop tables, p. 66

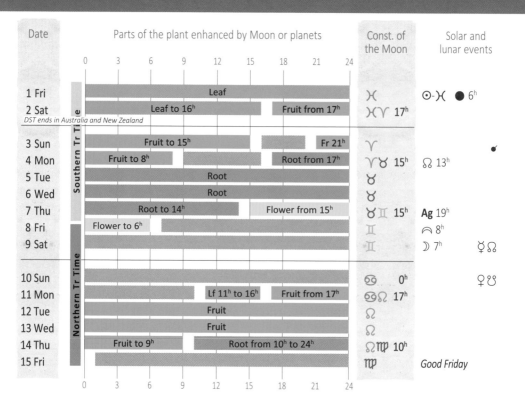

Date	Parts of the plant enhanced by Moon or planets	Const. of the Moon	Solar and lunar events
1 Fri	Leaf	♓	☉-♓ ● 6ʰ
2 Sat	Leaf to 16ʰ — Fruit from 17ʰ	♓♈ 17ʰ	
DST ends in Australia and New Zealand			
3 Sun	Fruit to 15ʰ — Fr 21ʰ	♈	
4 Mon	Fruit to 8ʰ — Root from 17ʰ	♈♉ 15ʰ	☊ 13ʰ
5 Tue	Root	♉	
6 Wed	Root	♉	
7 Thu	Root to 14ʰ — Flower from 15ʰ	♉♊ 15ʰ	**Ag** 19ʰ
8 Fri	Flower to 6ʰ	♊	⌢ 8ʰ
9 Sat		♊	☽ 7ʰ ☿☊
10 Sun		♋ 0ʰ	♀☋
11 Mon	Lf 11ʰ to 16ʰ — Fruit from 17ʰ	♋♌ 17ʰ	
12 Tue	Fruit	♌	
13 Wed	Fruit	♌	
14 Thu	Fruit to 9ʰ — Root from 10ʰ to 24ʰ	♌♍ 10ʰ	
15 Fri		♍	*Good Friday*

Southern Tr Time (1–9), Northern Tr Time (10–15)

In UK/Ireland remember to add 1 hour for Daylight Saving Time

---

Transplanting Time
(time of descending Moon in northern hemisphere)
April 8 10ʰ to April 21 16ʰ

Leaf times
- Tend leafy plants (like lettuce) during these times.
- Transplant endives, lettuce, cabbage, Brussels sprouts.

Root times

- Tend root plants (carrots, potatoes) during these times.
- Sow turnips, swede (rutabaga).

Fruit times

- Tend fruit plants (beans, grains, tomatoes) during these times.
- **Graft fruiting shrubs** outside Transplanting Times: April 2 17ʰ to April 4 10ʰ, avoiding unfavourable times.
- Sow courgettes (zucchini) and squash.

Flower times

- Tend flowering plants (broccoli, roses) during these times.
- **Graft flowering shrubs** outside Transplanting Times: April 7 15ʰ to April 8 6ʰ.
- Plant annuals and flowering shrubs.
- Prune flowering shrubs that have flowered.

Soil
The **soil warms up** on April 11.

Date	My notes	Planetary aspects (**Bold** = visible to naked eye)

Planet positions in zodiac

☿	Mercury	♓ 10 ♈
♀	Venus	♑ 2 ♒
♂	Mars	♑ 10 ♒
♃	Jupiter	♒ 2 ♓
♄	Saturn	♑
♅	Uranus	♈
♆	Neptune	♓
♇	Pluto	♐

Date	Planetary aspects
1	☽ ☌ ☿ 3^h
2	☉ ☌ ☿ 23^h
3	☽ ● ☝ 18^h
4	
5	♂ ☌ ♄ 2^h
6	
7	
8	
9	☿ ☋ 7^h
10	☽ ☍ ♇ 1^h ♀ ☋ 22^h
11	
12	☽ ☍ ♄ 1^h ☽ ☍ ♂ 10^h ♃ ☌ ♆ 15^h
13	☽ ☍ ♀ 5^h
14	☽ ☍ ♆ 10^h ☽ ☍ ♃ 11^h
15	

Planet (naked eye) visibility

Evening:
Mercury (from April 13)

All night: −

Morning:
Venus, Mars,
Jupiter (from April 14),
Saturn

♓ Pisces	♈ Aries	♉ Taurus	♊ Gemini	♋ Cancer	♌ Leo
♍ Virgo	♎ Libra	♏ Scorpio	♐ Sagittarius	♑ Capricorn	♒ Aquarius

NB: All zodiac symbols refer to astronomical constellations, not astrological signs (see p. 10)

Control pests
(see p. 74 for details)

- **Slugs:** ash from April 10 0^h to April 11 16^h.
- **Clothes and wax moths:** ash from March 30 19^h to April 2 16^h.

Good Friday and Easter

Maria Thun's research has shown that planting and other work is unfavourable from Good Friday to dawn on Easter Sunday, *local time*.

My notes

Southern hemisphere

Southern Transplanting Time
March 25 to April 8 6^h and April 21 20^h to May 5

Harvest time for seeds (*Avoid unfavourable times*)
- **Fruit seeds:** April 2 17^h to April 4 8^h and April 11 17^h to April 14 9^h.
- **Flower seeds:** April 7 15^h to April 8 6^h.
- **Leaf seeds:** March 30 19^h to April 2 16^h and April 11 11^h to 16^h.
- **Root seeds:** April 4 17^h to April 7 14^h and April 14 from 10^h to 24^h *local time*.

Control slugs from April 10 0^h to April 11 16^h.

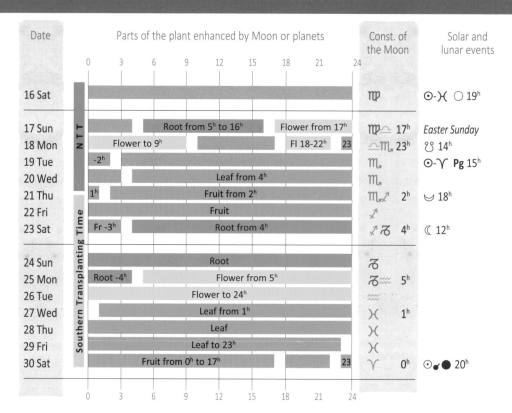

Date	Parts of the plant enhanced by Moon or planets	Const. of the Moon	Solar and lunar events
16 Sat		♍	☉-♓ ○ 19ʰ
17 Sun	Root from 5ʰ to 16ʰ — Flower from 17ʰ	♍♎ 17ʰ	*Easter Sunday*
18 Mon	Flower to 9ʰ — Fl 18-22ʰ 23	♎♏ 23ʰ	☋ 14ʰ
19 Tue	-2ʰ	♏	☉-♈ Pg 15ʰ
20 Wed	Leaf from 4ʰ	♏	
21 Thu	1ʰ Fruit from 2ʰ	♏♐ 2ʰ	☋ 18ʰ
22 Fri	Fruit	♐	
23 Sat	Fr -3ʰ Root from 4ʰ	♐♑ 4ʰ	☽ 12ʰ
24 Sun	Root	♑	
25 Mon	Root -4ʰ Flower from 5ʰ	♑♒ 5ʰ	
26 Tue	Flower to 24ʰ	♒	
27 Wed	Leaf from 1ʰ	♓ 1ʰ	
28 Thu	Leaf	♓	
29 Fri	Leaf to 23ʰ	♓	
30 Sat	Fruit from 0ʰ to 17ʰ 23	♈ 0ʰ	☉ ● 20ʰ

(Left margin: N T T — Southern Transplanting Time)

(Right margin: In UK/Ireland remember to add 1 hour for Daylight Saving Time)

Transplanting Time
(time of descending Moon in northern hemisphere)
April 8 to April 21 16ʰ

Leaf times

- Tend leafy plants (like lettuce) during these times.
- Mow lawns if you want to encourage vigorous growth of the grass.
- Transplant chicory, endives, cabbage, Brussels sprouts.

Root times

- Tend root plants (carrots, potatoes) during these times.
- Transplant **seed potatoes** for next year with Moon in Aries, from April 30 0ʰ to May 1 15ʰ, avoiding unfavourable times.
- Sow salsify and parsnips.

Fruit times

- Tend fruit plants (beans, grains, tomatoes) during these times.
- **Graft fruiting shrubs** outside Transplanting Times: April 21 20ʰ to April 23 3ʰ and April 30 0ʰ to May 1 15ʰ, avoiding unfavourable times.
- Transplant aubergines (eggplant), tomatoes.

Flower times

- Tend flowering plants (broccoli, roses) during these times.
- **Graft flowering shrubs** outside Transplanting Times: April 25 5ʰ to April 26 24ʰ.
- Transplant cauliflowers and broccoli.
- Plant begonias, dahlias, gladiolas and other annual flowers.

APRIL 16–30, 2022

Date	My notes	Planetary aspects (**Bold** = visible to naked eye)
16		
17		☾☍☿ 23^h
18		☿☌♅ 5^h ☾☍♅ 23^h
19		
20		
21		
22		
23		☾☌♇ 4^h
24		
25		**☾☌♄ 0^h**
26		**☾☌♂ 1^h**
27		**☾☌♀ 5^h** ☾☌♆ 6^h **☾☌♃ 11^h** ♀☌♆ 19^h
28		☿△♇ 12^h
29		
30		**♀☌♃ 21^h**

Planet positions in zodiac

☿ Mercury	♈ 24 ♉
♀ Venus	♒ 25 ♓
♂ Mars	♒
♃ Jupiter	♓
♄ Saturn	♑
♅ Uranus	♈
♆ Neptune	♓
♇ Pluto	♐ (29 R)

Planet (naked eye) visibility

Evening:
Mercury

All night:
–

Morning:
Venus, Mars, Jupiter, Saturn

♓ Pisces ♈ Aries ♉ Taurus ♊ Gemini ♋ Cancer ♌ Leo
♍ Virgo ♎ Libra ♏ Scorpio ♐ Sagittarius ♑ Capricorn ♒ Aquarius

NB: All zodiac symbols refer to astronomical constellations, not astrological signs (see p. 10)

Control pests
(see p. 74 for details)

- **Clothes and wax moths:** ash from April 27 1^h to April 29 23^h.

Biodynamic preparations

Preparations can be taken out of the ground after April 18 avoiding unfavourable times (best at Fruit or Flower times). Preparations put into the ground after Sep 15, 2021 should wait until the end of May.

Good Friday and Easter

Maria Thun's research has shown that planting and other work is unfavourable from Good Friday to dawn on Easter Sunday, *local time.*

Southern hemisphere

Southern Transplanting Time
April 21 20^h to May 5

Harvest time for seeds *(*Avoid unfavourable times)*

- **Fruit seeds:** April 21 2^h to April 23 3^h and April 30 0^h to May 1 15^h.*
- **Flower seeds:** April 17 17^h to April 18 22^h.*
- **Leaf seeds:** April 20 4^h to April 21 1^h and April 27 1^h to April 29 23^h.
- **Root seeds:** April 17 dawn to 16^h and April 23 4^h to April 25 4^h.

MAY 1–15, 2022

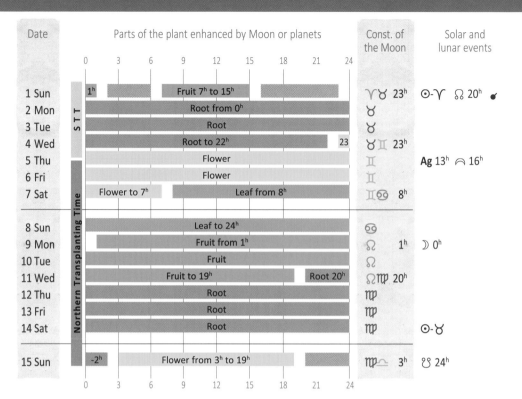

Date		Parts of the plant enhanced by Moon or planets	Const. of the Moon	Solar and lunar events
1 Sun	STT	1^h / Fruit 7^h to 15^h	♈♉ 23^h	☉-♈ ☊ 20^h ●
2 Mon	STT	Root from 0^h	♉	
3 Tue	STT	Root	♉	
4 Wed	STT	Root to 22^h / 23	♉♊ 23^h	
5 Thu	Northern Transplanting Time	Flower	♊	**Ag** 13^h ⋒ 16^h
6 Fri	Northern Transplanting Time	Flower	♊	
7 Sat	Northern Transplanting Time	Flower to 7^h / Leaf from 8^h	♊♋ 8^h	
8 Sun	Northern Transplanting Time	Leaf to 24^h	♋	
9 Mon	Northern Transplanting Time	Fruit from 1^h	♌ 1^h	☽ 0^h
10 Tue	Northern Transplanting Time	Fruit	♌	
11 Wed	Northern Transplanting Time	Fruit to 19^h / Root 20^h	♌♍ 20^h	
12 Thu	Northern Transplanting Time	Root	♍	
13 Fri	Northern Transplanting Time	Root	♍	
14 Sat	Northern Transplanting Time	Root	♍	☉-♉
15 Sun	Northern Transplanting Time	-2^h / Flower from 3^h to 19^h	♍♎ 3^h	☋ 24^h

In UK/Ireland remember to add 1 hour for Daylight Saving Time

Transplanting Time
(time of descending Moon in northern hemisphere)
May 5 18^h to May 18 23^h

Leaf times

- Tend leafy plants (like lettuce) during these times.
- Plant aromatic herbs.
- Transplant cabbage.
- Sow lettuce, endives, parsley, chervil, kale.

Root times

- Tend root plants (carrots, potatoes) during these times.
- Transplant **table potatoes**.
- Transplant **seed potatoes** for next year with Moon in Aries, from April 30 0^h to May 1 15^h, avoiding unfavourable times.
- Sow beetroots (beets) and carrots.

Fruit times

- Tend fruit plants (beans, grains, tomatoes) during these times.
- **Graft fruiting shrubs** outside Transplanting Times: April 30 0^h to May 1 15^h, avoiding unfavourable times.
- Sow beans, courgettes (zucchini), cucumbers.

Flower times

- Tend flowering plants (broccoli, roses) during these times.
- Cut **hay** between May 4 23^h and May 7 7^h, and at other Flower times.
- Sow cauliflower and broccoli.

Beekeeping

Begin **queen bee** rearing (grafting or larval transfer, comb insertion, cell punching) between May 4 23^h and May 7 7^h and at other Flower times.

Date	My notes	Planetary aspects

(Bold = visible to naked eye)

Planet positions in zodiac

☿ Mercury ♉ (10 R)
♀ Venus ♓
♂ Mars ♒ 13 ♓
♃ Jupiter ♓
♄ Saturn ♑
♅ Uranus ♈
♆ Neptune ♓
♇ Pluto ♐ (R)

1 _____ ☽ ● ⚷ 4ʰ
2 _____ ☽ ☌ ☿ 15ʰ
3 _____
4 _____
5 _____ ☉ ☌ ⚷ 7ʰ
6 _____
7 _____ ☽ ☍ ♇ 9ʰ
  _____
8 _____
9 _____ ☽ ☍ ♄ 13ʰ
10 _____
11 _____ ☽ ☍ ♂ 12ʰ ☽ ☍ ♆ 21ʰ
12 _____ ☽ ☍ ♃ 7ʰ
13 _____ ☽ ☍ ♀ 4ʰ
14 _____
15 _____ ☽ ☍ ⚷ 12ʰ

Planet (naked eye) visibility

Evening:
  Mercury (to May 11)

All night:
  —

Morning:
  Venus, Mars, Jupiter, Saturn

♓ Pisces	♈ Aries	♉ Taurus	♊ Gemini	♋ Cancer	♌ Leo
♍ Virgo	♎ Libra	♏ Scorpio	♐ Sagittarius	♑ Capricorn	♒ Aquarius

NB: All zodiac symbols refer to astronomical constellations, not astrological signs (see p. 10)

Control pests
(see p. 74 for details)

- **Flies:** burn fly papers in the cow barn at Flower times.
- **Chitinous insects, wheat weevil, Colorado beetle and varroa:** ash from May 1 23ʰ to May 4 22ʰ.

Southern hemisphere

Southern Transplanting Time
April 21 to May 5 14ʰ and May 19 3ʰ to June 1

My notes

_____
_____
_____
_____
_____
_____
_____
_____

My notes

_____
_____
_____
_____
_____
_____
_____
_____
_____

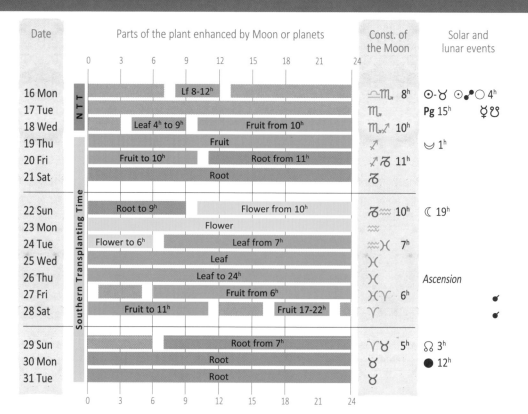

Date	Parts of the plant enhanced by Moon or planets	Const. of the Moon	Solar and lunar events
16 Mon	Lf 8-12^h	♎︎♏︎ 8^h	☉-♉ ☉🜨○ 4^h
17 Tue		♏︎	**Pg** 15^h ☿ ☋
18 Wed	Leaf 4^h to 9^h — Fruit from 10^h	♏︎♐︎ 10^h	
19 Thu	Fruit	♐︎	◡ 1^h
20 Fri	Fruit to 10^h — Root from 11^h	♐︎♑︎ 11^h	
21 Sat	Root	♑︎	
22 Sun	Root to 9^h — Flower from 10^h	♑︎♒︎ 10^h	☽ 19^h
23 Mon	Flower	♒︎	
24 Tue	Flower to 6^h — Leaf from 7^h	♒︎♓︎ 7^h	
25 Wed	Leaf	♓︎	
26 Thu	Leaf to 24^h	♓︎	*Ascension*
27 Fri	Fruit from 6^h	♓︎♈︎ 6^h	
28 Sat	Fruit to 11^h — Fruit 17-22^h	♈︎	
29 Sun	Root from 7^h	♈︎♉︎ 5^h	♋ 3^h
30 Mon	Root	♉︎	● 12^h
31 Tue	Root	♉︎	

N T T

Southern Transplanting Time

In UK/Ireland remember to add 1 hour for Daylight Saving Time

---

Transplanting Time
(time of descending Moon in northern hemisphere)
May 5 to May 18 23^h

Leaf times

- Tend leafy plants (like lettuce) during these times.
- Prune hedges.
- Transplant Brussels sprouts, celery, lettuce.
- Thin lettuce and chard.

Root times

- Tend root plants (carrots, potatoes) during these times.
- Transplant **table potatoes.**
- Transplant **seed potatoes** for next year from May 27 6^h to May 28 22^h, avoiding unfavourable times.
- Sow winter radishes and carrots.

Fruit times

- Tend fruit plants (beans, grains, tomatoes) during these times.
- Prune suckers off tomatoes, cucumbers.
- Prune fruit trees after the fruit falls off.

Flower times

- Tend flowering plants (broccoli, roses) during these times.
- Cut **hay** between May 22 10^h and May 24 6^h, and at other Flower times.
- Layer climbing roses, clematis, honeysuckle.

Beekeeping
- Begin **queen bee** rearing (grafting or larval transfer, comb insertion, cell punching) at Flower times.
- Make and sprinkle **varroa ash** between May 29 5^h and June 1 4^h.

Date	My notes	Planetary aspects
		(**Bold** = visible to naked eye)

Date	Planetary aspects
16	☾ ☌ ☿ 17ʰ
17	☿ ☊ 13ʰ
18	♂ ☌ ♆ 7ʰ
19	☉ △ ♇ 12ʰ
20	☾ ☌ ♇ 10ʰ
21	☉ ☌ ☿ 19ʰ
22	☾ ☌ ♄ 7ʰ
23	
24	☾ ☌ ♆ 13ʰ ☾ ☌ ♂ 22ʰ
25	☾ ☌ ♃ 2ʰ ☿ △ ♇ 22ʰ
26	
27	☾ ☌ ♀ 3ʰ
28	☾ ☌ ♁ 14ʰ
29	♂ ☌ ♃ 11ʰ ☾ ☌ ☿ 11ʰ
30	
31	

Planet positions in zodiac

☿	Mercury	♉ (R)
♀	Venus	♓ 28 ♈
♂	Mars	♓
♃	Jupiter	♓
♄	Saturn	♑
♅	Uranus	♈
♆	Neptune	♓
♇	Pluto	♐ (R)

Planet (naked eye) visibility

Evening:
–

All night:
–

Morning:
Venus, Mars, Jupiter, Saturn

♓ Pisces	♈ Aries	♉ Taurus	♊ Gemini	♋ Cancer	♌ Leo
♍ Virgo	♎ Libra	♏ Scorpio	♐ Sagittarius	♑ Capricorn	♒ Aquarius

Control pests
(see p. 74 for details)

- **Flies:** burn fly papers in the cow barn at Flower times.
- **Moths:** ash from May 24 7ʰ to May 27 5ʰ.
- **Mole crickets:** ash from May 16 8ʰ to May 18 9ʰ.
- **Chitinous insects, wheat weevil, Colorado beetle and varroa:** ash from May 29 5ʰ to June 1 4ʰ.

Southern hemisphere

Southern Transplanting Time
May 19 3ʰ to June 1

My notes

My notes

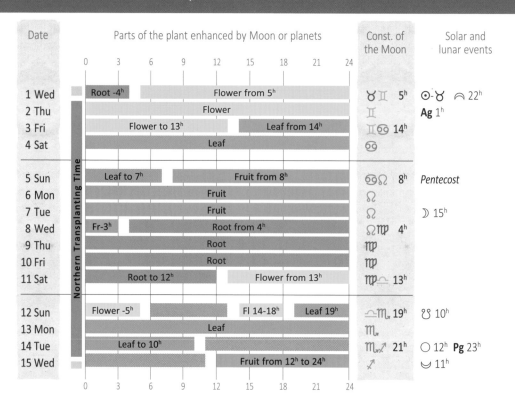

Date	Parts of the plant enhanced by Moon or planets	Const. of the Moon	Solar and lunar events
1 Wed	Root -4ʰ / Flower from 5ʰ	♉♊ 5ʰ	☉-♉ ⌒ 22ʰ
2 Thu	Flower	♊	**Ag** 1ʰ
3 Fri	Flower to 13ʰ / Leaf from 14ʰ	♊♋ 14ʰ	
4 Sat	Leaf	♋	
5 Sun	Leaf to 7ʰ / Fruit from 8ʰ	♋♌ 8ʰ	*Pentecost*
6 Mon	Fruit	♌	
7 Tue	Fruit	♌	☽ 15ʰ
8 Wed	Fr-3ʰ / Root from 4ʰ	♌♍ 4ʰ	
9 Thu	Root	♍	
10 Fri	Root	♍	
11 Sat	Root to 12ʰ / Flower from 13ʰ	♍⌒ 13ʰ	
12 Sun	Flower -5ʰ / Fl 14-18ʰ / Leaf 19ʰ	⌒♏ 19ʰ	☍ 10ʰ
13 Mon	Leaf	♏	
14 Tue	Leaf to 10ʰ	♏♐ 21ʰ	○ 12ʰ **Pg** 23ʰ
15 Wed	Fruit from 12ʰ to 24ʰ	♐	☋ 11ʰ

Northern Transplanting Time

In UK/Ireland remember to add 1 hour for Daylight Saving Time

---

Transplanting Time
(time of descending Moon in northern hemisphere)
June 2 0ʰ to June 15 9ʰ and June 29 6ʰ to July 12

Fruit times
- Tend fruit plants (beans, grains, tomatoes) during these times.
- Sow beans, cucumbers, courgettes (zucchini).

Leaf times

- Tend leafy plants (like lettuce) during these times.
- Thin and/or transplant any lettuce, Brussels sprouts, cabbage, kale, etc. that need it.
- Cut aromatic herbs before they bloom.

Flower times

- Tend flowering plants (broccoli, roses) during these times.
- Cut **hay.**
- Pick flowers for teas and dry them in the dark.
- Layer wisteria and trumpet vines.
- Thin or transplant cauliflowers, broccoli.

Root times

- Tend root plants (carrots, potatoes) during these times.
- Sow winter radishes, swedes (rutabaga), parsnips and carrots for autumn harvesting.

Beekeeping
Begin **queen bee** rearing (grafting or larval transfer, comb insertion, cell punching) at Flower times.

Date	My notes	Planetary aspects (**Bold** = visible to naked eye)

1 _____

2 _____

3 _____ $\mathbb{D} \, \sigma^o \, ♇ \; 15^h$

4 _____

5 _____ $\mathbb{D} \, \sigma^o \, ♄ \; 21^h$

6 _____

7 _____

8 _____ $\mathbb{D} \, \sigma^o \, ♆ \; 7^h$

9 _____ $\mathbb{D} \, \sigma^o \, ♃ \; 0^h \quad \mathbb{D} \, \sigma^o \, ♂ \; 12^h$

10 _____ $☿ \, \triangle \, ♇ \; 21^h$

11 _____ $♀ \, \sigma \, ⛢ \; 23^h$

12 _____ $\mathbb{D} \, \sigma^o \, ⛢ \; 1^h \quad \mathbb{D} \, \sigma^o \, ♀ \; 1^h \quad \mathbb{D} \, \sigma^o \, ☿ \; 22^h$

13 _____

14 _____

15 _____

Planet positions in zodiac

☿	Mercury	♉	(R 3 D)
♀	Venus	♈	
♂	Mars	♓	
♃	Jupiter	♓	
♄	Saturn	♑	(4 R)
⛢	Uranus	♈	
♆	Neptune	♓	
♇	Pluto	♐	(R)

Planet (naked eye) visibility

Evening:
—

All night:
Saturn

Morning:
Venus, Mars, Jupiter

♓ Pisces	♈ Aries	♉ Taurus	♊ Gemini	♋ Cancer	♌ Leo
♍ Virgo	♎ Libra	♏ Scorpio	♐ Sagittarius	♑ Capricorn	♒ Aquarius

NB: All zodiac symbols refer to astronomical constellations, not astrological signs (see p. 10)

Control pests
(see p. 74 for details)

- **Chitinous insects, wheat weevil, Colorado beetle and varroa:** ash from May 29 5^h to June 1 4^h.
- **Flies:** burn fly papers at Flower times.
- **Mole crickets:** ash from June 12 19^h to June 14 20^h.
- **Ants** in the house: ash when the Moon is in Leo, June 5 8^h to June 8 3^h.

Southern hemisphere

Southern Transplanting Time
May 19 to June 1 20^h
and June 15 13^h to June 29 2^h

My notes

_____
_____
_____
_____
_____
_____

My notes

_____
_____
_____
_____
_____

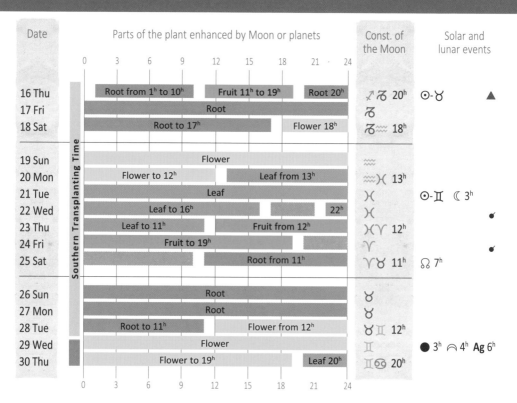

Date	Parts of the plant enhanced by Moon or planets	Const. of the Moon	Solar and lunar events
16 Thu	Root from 1ʰ to 10ʰ — Fruit 11ʰ to 19ʰ — Root 20ʰ	♐ ♑ 20ʰ	☉-♉ ▲
17 Fri	Root	♑	
18 Sat	Root to 17ʰ — Flower 18ʰ	♑ ♒ 18ʰ	
19 Sun	Flower	♒	
20 Mon	Flower to 12ʰ — Leaf from 13ʰ	♒ ♓ 13ʰ	
21 Tue	Leaf	♓	☉-♊ ☽ 3ʰ
22 Wed	Leaf to 16ʰ — 22ʰ	♓	
23 Thu	Leaf to 11ʰ — Fruit from 12ʰ	♓ ♈ 12ʰ	
24 Fri	Fruit to 19ʰ	♈	
25 Sat	Root from 11ʰ	♈ ♉ 11ʰ	☍ 7ʰ
26 Sun	Root	♉	
27 Mon	Root	♉	
28 Tue	Root to 11ʰ — Flower from 12ʰ	♉ ♊ 12ʰ	
29 Wed	Flower	♊	● 3ʰ ⌢ 4ʰ **Ag** 6ʰ
30 Thu	Flower to 19ʰ — Leaf 20ʰ	♊ ♋ 20ʰ	

Southern Transplanting Time (label at left of chart, rows 16–25)

In UK/Ireland remember to add 1 hour for Daylight Saving Time

---

Transplanting Time
(time of descending Moon in northern hemisphere)
June 29 6ʰ to July 12

Leaf times

- Tend leafy plants (like lettuce) during these times.
- Cut aromatic herbs before they bloom.
- Mow lawns if you want to encourage vigorous growth of the grass.

Root times

- Tend root plants (carrots, potatoes) during these times.
- Harvest early potatoes as needed.
- Harvest onions, garlic, shallots, and dry before storing.

Fruit times

- Tend fruit plants (beans, grains, tomatoes) during these times.
- Harvest tomatoes.
- Sow courgettes (zucchini).
- Lightly prune fruit trees and shrubs.

Flower times

- Tend flowering plants (broccoli, roses) during these times.
- Cut **hay.**

Beekeeping
Begin **queen bee** rearing (grafting or larval transfer, comb insertion, cell punching) at Flower times.

Date	My notes	Planetary aspects (**Bold** = visible to naked eye)

Planet positions in zodiac

☿ Mercury ♉
♀ Venus ♈ 17 ♉
♂ Mars ♓
♃ Jupiter ♓
♄ Saturn ♑ (R)
⛢ Uranus ♈
♆ Neptune ♓ (28 R)
♇ Pluto ♐ (R)

Date	Planetary aspects
16	⊙△♄ 7ʰ ☾☌♇ 19ʰ
17	
18	☾☌♄ 15ʰ
19	
20	☾☌♆ 19ʰ
21	♀△♇ 8ʰ ☾☌♃ 16ʰ
22	☾•☌♂ 19ʰ
23	
24	☾•☌⛢ 22ʰ
25	
26	☾☌♀ 7ʰ
27	☾☌☿ 7ʰ
28	
29	
30	☽☌☍♇ 20ʰ

Planet (naked eye) visibility

Evening:
–

All night:
Saturn

Morning:
Venus, Mars, Jupiter

♓ Pisces   ♈ Aries   ♉ Taurus   ♊ Gemini   ♋ Cancer   ♌ Leo
♍ Virgo   ♎ Libra   ♏ Scorpio   ♐ Sagittarius   ♑ Capricorn   ♒ Aquarius

NB: All zodiac symbols refer to astronomical constellations, not astrological signs (see p. 10)

Control pests
(see p. 74 for details)

- **Chitinous insects, wheat weevil, Colorado beetle and varroa:** ash from June 25 11ʰ to June 28 11ʰ.
- **Flies:** burn fly papers at Flower times.
- **Grasshoppers:** ash from June 18 18ʰ to June 20 12ʰ, and June 28 12ʰ to June 30 19ʰ.

Biodynamic preparations
Look for the places where **valerian** is growing to save time searching for it when it comes to harvesting in July and August.

Tip
Want to know more about biodynamic preparations?
- See Biodynamic preparations, p. 73

Southern hemisphere
Southern Transplanting Time
June 15 to June 29 2ʰ

My notes

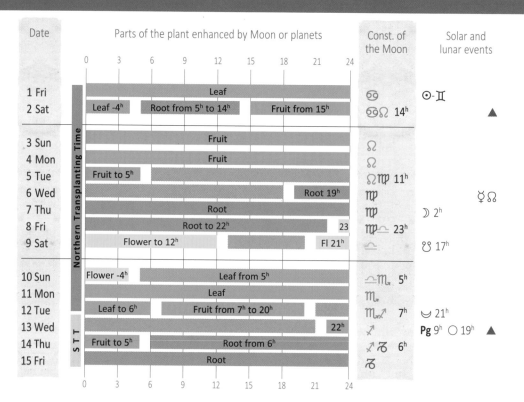

Date	Parts of the plant enhanced by Moon or planets	Const. of the Moon	Solar and lunar events
1 Fri	Leaf	♋♋	☉–♊
2 Sat	Leaf -4ʰ / Root from 5ʰ to 14ʰ / Fruit from 15ʰ	♋♋♌ 14ʰ	▲
3 Sun	Fruit	♌	
4 Mon	Fruit	♌	
5 Tue	Fruit to 5ʰ	♌♍ 11ʰ	
6 Wed	Root 19ʰ	♍	☿ ♌
7 Thu	Root	♍	☽ 2ʰ
8 Fri	Root to 22ʰ / 23	♍♎ 23ʰ	
9 Sat	Flower to 12ʰ / Fl 21ʰ	♎	☍ 17ʰ
10 Sun	Flower -4ʰ / Leaf from 5ʰ	♎♏ 5ʰ	
11 Mon	Leaf	♏	
12 Tue	Leaf to 6ʰ / Fruit from 7ʰ to 20ʰ	♏♐ 7ʰ	☌ 21ʰ
13 Wed	22ʰ	♐	Pg 9ʰ ○ 19ʰ ▲
14 Thu	Fruit to 5ʰ / Root from 6ʰ	♐♑ 6ʰ	
15 Fri	Root	♑	

Northern Transplanting Time (1 Fri – 12 Tue), *S T T* (13 Wed – 15 Fri)

In UK/Ireland remember to add 1 hour for Daylight Saving Time

---

Transplanting Time
(time of descending Moon in northern hemisphere)
June 29 to July 12 19ʰ and July 26 11ʰ to Aug 9

Leaf times

- Tend leafy plants (like lettuce) during these times.
- Harvest **seeds of leaf plants** to be used for seed from June 30 20ʰ to July 2 4ʰ and at other Leaf times, avoiding unfavourable times.
- Spray leaf plants and the soil with horn silica early in the morning.

Root times

- Tend root plants (carrots, potatoes) during these times.
- Harvest **seeds of root plants** to be used for seed from July 6 19ʰ to July 8 22ʰ and at other Root times, avoiding unfavourable times.

Fruit times
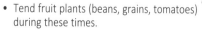
- Tend fruit plants (beans, grains, tomatoes) during these times.
- Harvest **seeds of fruit plants** and **grain** to be used for seed from July 2 15ʰ to July 5 5ʰ and at other Fruit times, avoiding unfavourable times.
- Sow climbing and runner (pole) beans.
- Prune tomato suckers or side shoots.

Flower times

- Tend flowering plants (broccoli, roses) during these times.
- Harvest **seeds of flower plants** to be used for seed from July 8 23ʰ to July 10 4ʰ and at other Flower times, avoiding unfavourable times.
- Cut **late hay.**
- Sow biennials such as pansies, and perenniels like hyssop, columbine, etc.

Date	My notes	Planetary aspects (**Bold** = visible to naked eye)

Planetary aspects
(**Bold** = visible to naked eye)

1
2      $☿△♄$ 11^h

3      $☽☍♄$ 2^h
4
5      $☽☍♆$ 14^h
6      $☿☊$ 6^h $☽☍♃$ 13^h
7
8      $☽☍♂$ 9^h
9      $☽☍♅$ 13^h

10
11      $☽☍♀$ 21^h
12
13      $♀△♄$ 5^h $☽☍☿$ 12^h
14      $☾☌♇$ 4^h
15      $☾☌♄$ 22^h

Planet positions in zodiac

☿	Mercury	♉ 5 ♊
♀	Venus	♉
♂	Mars	♓ 4 ♈
♃	Jupiter	♓
♄	Saturn	♑ (R)
♅	Uranus	♈
♆	Neptune	♓ (R)
♇	Pluto	♐ (R)

Planet (naked eye) visibility

Evening:
–

All night:
Saturn

Morning:
Venus, Mars, Jupiter

♓ Pisces	♈ Aries	♉ Taurus	♊ Gemini	♋ Cancer	♌ Leo
♍ Virgo	♎ Libra	♏ Scorpio	♐ Sagittarius	♑ Capricorn	♒ Aquarius

NB: All zodiac symbols refer to astronomical constellations, not astrological signs (see p. 10)

Control pests
(see p. 74 for details)

- **Flies:** burn fly papers at Flower times.
- **Slugs:** ash from June 30 20^h to July 2 4^h. Spray leaf plants and the soil with horn silica early in the morning during Leaf times.
- **Ants** in the house: ash when the Moon is in Leo, July 2 14^h to July 5 10^h.

Southern hemisphere
Southern Transplanting Time
July 12 23^h to July 26 7^h

My notes

Biodynamic preparations

Pick **valerian** flowers at Flower times early in the morning while there is still plenty of night-time moisture around. The juice should be pressed out immediately without adding any water or leaving the plants in water. Juice to which water has been added will not keep long.

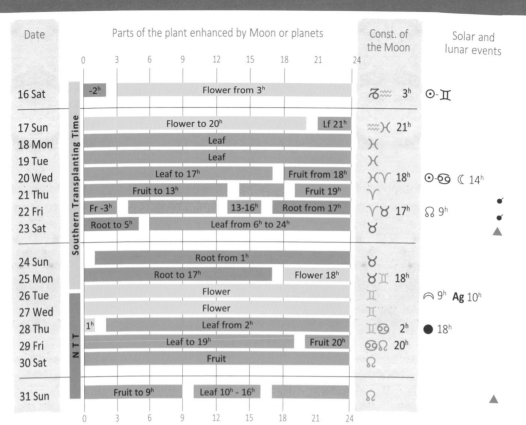

Date	Parts of the plant enhanced by Moon or planets	Const. of the Moon	Solar and lunar events
16 Sat	-2ʰ Flower from 3ʰ	♑ ♒ 3ʰ	☉-♊
17 Sun	Flower to 20ʰ Lf 21ʰ	♒ ♓ 21ʰ	
18 Mon	Leaf	♓	
19 Tue	Leaf	♓	
20 Wed	Leaf to 17ʰ Fruit from 18ʰ	♓ ♈ 18ʰ	☉-♋ ☾ 14ʰ
21 Thu	Fruit to 13ʰ Fruit 19ʰ	♈	
22 Fri	Fr -3ʰ 13-16ʰ Root from 17ʰ	♈ ♉ 17ʰ	☍ 9ʰ
23 Sat	Root to 5ʰ Leaf from 6ʰ to 24ʰ	♉	▲
24 Sun	Root from 1ʰ	♉	
25 Mon	Root to 17ʰ Flower 18ʰ	♉ ♊ 18ʰ	
26 Tue	Flower	♊	⌒ 9ʰ Ag 10ʰ
27 Wed	Flower	♊	
28 Thu	1ʰ Leaf from 2ʰ	♊ ♋ 2ʰ	● 18ʰ
29 Fri	Leaf to 19ʰ Fruit 20ʰ	♋ ♌ 20ʰ	
30 Sat	Fruit	♌	
31 Sun	Fruit to 9ʰ Leaf 10ʰ - 16ʰ	♌	▲

Southern Transplanting Time (16–23)

NTT (28–31)

In UK/Ireland remember to add 1 hour for Daylight Saving Time

---

Transplanting Time
(time of descending Moon in northern hemisphere)
July 26 11ʰ to Aug 9

Leaf times
- Tend leafy plants (like lettuce) during these times.
- Harvest **seeds of leaf plants** to be used for seed from July 17 21ʰ to July 20 17ʰ.
- Spray leaf plants and the soil with horn silica early in the morning.

Root times
- Tend root plants (carrots, potatoes) during these times.
- Harvest **seeds of root plants** to be used for seed from July 22 17ʰ to July 23 5ʰ and July 24 1ʰ to July 25 17ʰ.

Fruit times
- Tend fruit plants (beans, grains, tomatoes) during these times.
- Harvest **seeds of fruit plants** and **grain** to be used for seed from July 29 20ʰ to July 31 9ʰ and at other Fruit times, avoiding unfavourable times.
- Cut raspberry canes that have finished bearing fruit.

Flower times
- Tend flowering plants (broccoli, roses) during these times.
- Harvest **seeds of flower plants** to be used for seed from July 25 18ʰ to July 28 1ʰ and at other Flower times, avoiding unfavourable times.
- Cut **late hay.**
- Plant autumn flowering bulbs.
- Graft rosehips.

Date	My notes	Planetary aspects
		(**Bold** = visible to naked eye)

Date	My notes	Planetary aspects
16		☉☌☿ 20ʰ
17		☿△♆ 8ʰ ☉△♆ 23ʰ
18		☾☌♆ 3ʰ ☿☍♇ 7ʰ
19		**☾☌♃ 3ʰ**
20		☉☍♇ 1ʰ
21		**☾☌♂ 16ʰ**
22		**☾**☍♅ 6ʰ
23		☿△♃ 18ʰ
24		
25		
26		**☾☌♀ 15ʰ**
27		
28		☾☍♇ 1ʰ
29		
30		☽☌☿ 0ʰ ☽☍♄ 5ʰ
31		☿☍♄ 6ʰ ☉△♃ 22ʰ

Planet positions in zodiac

☿	Mercury	♊	18♋
			28♌
♀	Venus	♉	17♊
♂	Mars	♈	
♃	Jupiter	♓	(28 R)
♄	Saturn	♑	(R)
♅	Uranus	♈	
♆	Neptune	♓	(R)
♇	Pluto	♐	(R)

Planet (naked eye) visibility

Evening:
–

All night:
Saturn

Morning:
Venus, Mars, Jupiter

NB: All zodiac symbols refer to astronomical constellations, not astrological signs (see p. 10)

Control pests
(see p. 74 for details)

- **Flies:** burn fly papers at Flower times.
- **Slugs:** ash from July 28 2ʰ to July 29 19ʰ. Spray leaf plants and the soil with horn silica early in the morning during Leaf times.
- **Grasshoppers:** ash July 25 18ʰ to July 28 1ʰ.
- **Ants** in the house: ash when the Moon is in Leo, July 29 20ʰ to Aug 1 15ʰ.

Biodynamic preparations

Pick **Valerian** flowers at Flower times early in the morning while there is still plenty of night-time moisture around. The juice should be pressed out immediately without adding any water or leaving the plants in water. Juice to which water has been added will not keep long.

Southern hemisphere

Southern Transplanting Time
July 12 to July 26 7ʰ

Maria Thun's tree log preparations

- Cut **larch** logs, fill with dried **camomile** and put them into the ground between July 17 20ʰ and July 18 13ʰ or between July 30 19ʰ and July 31 12ʰ.
- Cut **maple** logs, fill with dried **dandelion** and put them into the ground between July 19 14ʰ and Juy 20 7ʰ.

Tip

Want to know more about biodynamic preparations?
- See Biodynamic preparations, p. 73

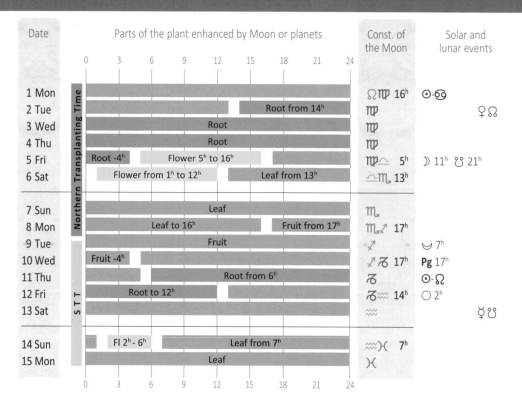

Date	Parts of the plant enhanced by Moon or planets	Const. of the Moon	Solar and lunar events
1 Mon	*(Northern Transplanting Time)*	♎︎♍︎ 16ʰ	☉-♋︎
2 Tue	Root from 14ʰ	♍︎	♀♌︎
3 Wed	Root	♍︎	
4 Thu	Root	♍︎	
5 Fri	Root -4ʰ · Flower 5ʰ to 16ʰ	♍︎♎︎ 5ʰ	☽ 11ʰ ☊ 21ʰ
6 Sat	Flower from 1ʰ to 12ʰ · Leaf from 13ʰ	♎︎♏︎ 13ʰ	
7 Sun	Leaf	♏︎	
8 Mon	Leaf to 16ʰ · Fruit from 17ʰ	♏︎♐︎ 17ʰ	
9 Tue	Fruit	♐︎	☽ 7ʰ
10 Wed	Fruit -4ʰ	♐︎♑︎ 17ʰ	Pg 17ʰ
11 Thu	Root from 6ʰ	♑︎	☉-♌︎
12 Fri	Root to 12ʰ	♑︎♒︎ 14ʰ	○ 2ʰ
13 Sat	*(STT)*	♒︎	☿♋︎
14 Sun	Fl 2ʰ - 6ʰ · Leaf from 7ʰ	♒︎♓︎ 7ʰ	
15 Mon	Leaf	♓︎	

In UK/Ireland remember to add 1 hour for Daylight Saving Time

---

Transplanting Time
(time of descending Moon in northern hemisphere)
July 26 to Aug 9 5ʰ and Aug 22 17ʰ to Sep 5

Leaf times
- Tend leafy plants (like lettuce) during these times.
- Harvest **seeds of leaf plants** to be used for seed from Aug 6 13ʰ to Aug 8 16ʰ and from Aug 14 7ʰ to Aug 16 5ʰ.
- Sow weather hardy lamb's lettuce and cabbage.

Root times
- Tend root plants (carrots, potatoes).
- Harvest **seeds of root plants** to be used for seed from Aug 2 14ʰ to Aug 5 4ʰ and from Aug 11 6ʰ to Aug 12 12ʰ.
- Harvest carrots, onions, potatoes.

Fruit times

- Tend fruit plants (beans, grains, tomatoes) during these times.
- Harvest **seeds of fruit plants** and **grain** to be used for seed from Aug 8 17ʰ to Aug 10 4ʰ and at other Fruit times, avoiding unfavourable times.
- Immediately after harvest, sow catch crops like lupins, phacelia, mustard or wild flax.
- After the harvest prune fruit trees.

Flower times

- Tend flowering plants (broccoli, roses) during these times.
- Harvest **seeds of flower plants** to be used for seed, but best in second half of the month, when there is a longer uninterrupted Flower time.
- Prune roses.

Date	My notes	Planetary aspects (**Bold** = visible to naked eye)

1	☽ ☌ ♆ 19ʰ
2	♂ ☌ ⚵ 0ʰ ♀ ☍ ♌ 1ʰ ☽ ☍ ♃ 20ʰ
3	
4	
5	☽ ☍ ⚵ 21ʰ
6	☽ ☍ ♂ 2ʰ
7	♀ △ ♆ 17ʰ
8	
9	♀ ☍ ♇ 5ʰ
10	☽ ☌ ♇ 14ʰ ☽ ☍ ♀ 17ʰ
11	
12	☾ ☌ ♄ 6ʰ
13	☿ ☍ 13ʰ ☾ ☍ ☿ 19ʰ
14	☾ ☌ ♆ 12ʰ ☉ ☍ ♄ 17ʰ ♂ △ ♇ 21ʰ
15	☾ ☌ ♃ 11ʰ

Planet positions in zodiac

☿	Mercury	♌
♀	Venus	♊ 9 ♋
♂	Mars	♈ 9 ♉
♃	Jupiter	♓ (R)
♄	Saturn	♑ (R)
⚵	Uranus	♈
♆	Neptune	♓ (R)
♇	Pluto	♐ (R)

Planet (naked eye) visibility

Evening:
  –

All night:
  Jupiter, Saturn

Morning:
  Venus, Mars

♓ Pisces	♈ Aries	♉ Taurus	♊ Gemini	♋ Cancer	♌ Leo
♍ Virgo	♎ Libra	♏ Scorpio	♐ Sagittarius	♑ Capricorn	♒ Aquarius

NB: All zodiac symbols refer to astronomical constellations, not astrological signs (see p. 10)

Control pests
(see p. 74 for details)
- **Flies:** burn fly papers at Flower times.
- **Ants** in the house: ash when the Moon is in Leo, July 29 20ʰ to Aug 1 15ʰ.

Maria Thun's tree log preparations
- Cut **birch** logs, fill with dried **yarrow** and put them into the ground between Aug 8 18ʰ and Aug 9 11ʰ.
- Cut **maple** logs, fill with dried **dandelion** and put them into the ground between Aug 14 6ʰ and 23ʰ.

Tip
Not sure what type of plant your vegetable is?
- See Crop tables, p. 66

Southern hemisphere
Southern Transplanting Time
Aug 9 9ʰ to Aug 22 13ʰ

My notes

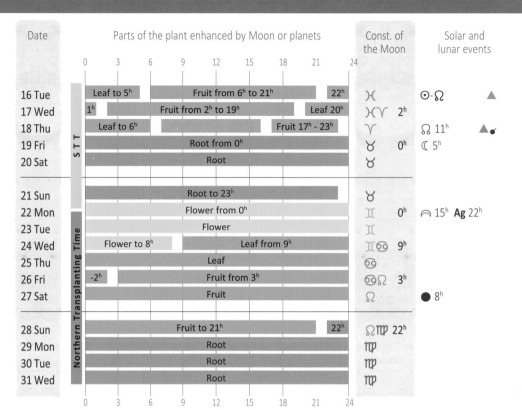

Date	Parts of the plant enhanced by Moon or planets	Const. of the Moon	Solar and lunar events
16 Tue	Leaf to 5ʰ · Fruit from 6ʰ to 21ʰ · 22ʰ	♓	☉-♌ ▲
17 Wed	1ʰ · Fruit from 2ʰ to 19ʰ · Leaf 20ʰ	♓♈ 2ʰ	
18 Thu	Leaf to 6ʰ · Fruit 17ʰ - 23ʰ	♈	♌ 11ʰ ▲ ☽
19 Fri	Root from 0ʰ	♉ 0ʰ	☾ 5ʰ
20 Sat	Root	♉	
21 Sun	Root to 23ʰ	♉	
22 Mon	Flower from 0ʰ	♊ 0ʰ	⌒ 15ʰ **Ag** 22ʰ
23 Tue	Flower	♊	
24 Wed	Flower to 8ʰ · Leaf from 9ʰ	♊♋ 9ʰ	
25 Thu	Leaf	♋	
26 Fri	-2ʰ · Fruit from 3ʰ	♋♌ 3ʰ	
27 Sat	Fruit	♌	● 8ʰ
28 Sun	Fruit to 21ʰ · 22ʰ	♌♍ 22ʰ	
29 Mon	Root	♍	
30 Tue	Root	♍	
31 Wed	Root	♍	

STT (Sowing and Transplanting Time)

Northern Transplanting Time

In UK/Ireland remember to add 1 hour for Daylight Saving Time

---

Transplanting Time
(time of descending Moon in northern hemisphere)
Aug 22 17ʰ to Sep 5

Leaf times

- Tend leafy plants (like lettuce) during these times.
- Harvest **seeds of leaf plants** to be used for seed from Aug 14 7ʰ to Aug 16 5ʰ and from Aug 24 9ʰ to Aug 26 2ʰ.
- Mow lawns if you want to encourage vigorous growth of the grass.

Root times

- Tend root plants (carrots, potatoes) during these times.
- Harvest **seeds of leaf plants** to be used for seed from Aug 19 0ʰ to Aug 21 23ʰ and from Aug 28 22ʰ to Sep 1 10ʰ.

Fruit times

- Tend fruit plants (beans, grains, tomatoes) during these times.
- Harvest **seeds of fruit plants** and **grain** to be used for seed from Aug 26 3ʰ to Aug 28 21ʰ and at other Fruit times, avoiding unfavourable times.
- Immediately after harvest, sow catch crops like lupins, phacelia, mustard or wild flax.

Flower times

- Tend flowering plants (broccoli, roses) during these times.
- Harvest **seeds of flower plants** to be used for seed from Aug 22 0ʰ to Aug 24 8ʰ.
- Sow hardy annuals for early bloom next spring.
- Graft rosehips.

Date	My notes	Planetary aspects (**Bold** = visible to naked eye)
16		☿△♅ 18^h
17		
18		♀△♃ 8^h ☾●♅ 14^h
19		**☾☌♂ 11^h**
20		
21		☿☍♆ 8^h
22		☿△♇ 22^h
23		
24		☾☍♇ 6^h
25		
26		**☾☌♀ 0^h** ☾☍♄ 7^h
27		
28		♀☍♄ 18^h ☽☍♆ 23^h
29		☽☌☿ 16^h ☽☍♃ 23^h
30		
31		

Planet positions in zodiac

☿ Mercury	♌	20 ♍
♀ Venus	♋	27 ♌
♂ Mars	♉	
♃ Jupiter	♓	(R)
♄ Saturn	♑	(R)
♅ Uranus	♈	(24 R)
♆ Neptune	♓	(R)
♇ Pluto	♐	(R)

Planet (naked eye) visibility

Evening:
–

All night:
Jupiter, Saturn

Morning:
Venus, Mars

♓ Pisces ♈ Aries ♉ Taurus ♊ Gemini ♋ Cancer ♌ Leo
♍ Virgo ♎ Libra ♏ Scorpio ♐ Sagittarius ♑ Capricorn ♒ Aquarius

Control pests
(see p. 74 for details)

- **Flies:** burn fly papers at Flower times.
- **Ants** in the house: ash when the Moon is in Leo, Aug 26 3^h to Aug 28 21^h.

Biodynamic preparations

Cut **yarrow** in the mornings at Fruit times. The blossoms should show some seed formation.

Maria Thun's tree log preparations

- Cut **larch** logs, fill with dried **camomile** and put them into the ground between Aug 20 21^h and Aug 21 14^h.
- Cut **birch** logs, fill with dried **yarrow** and put them into the ground on Aug 28 between 7^h and 24^h.

Southern hemisphere

Southern Transplanting Time
Aug 9 to Aug 22 13^h

My notes

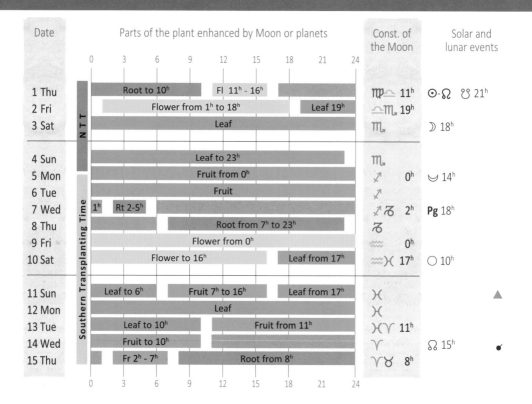

Date	Parts of the plant enhanced by Moon or planets	Const. of the Moon	Solar and lunar events
1 Thu	Root to 10ʰ / Fl 11ʰ – 16ʰ	♍︎♎︎ 11ʰ	☉-♌︎ ☋ 21ʰ
2 Fri	Flower from 1ʰ to 18ʰ / Leaf 19ʰ	♎︎♏︎ 19ʰ	
3 Sat	Leaf	♏︎	☽ 18ʰ
4 Sun	Leaf to 23ʰ	♏︎	
5 Mon	Fruit from 0ʰ	♐︎ 0ʰ	⚲ 14ʰ
6 Tue	Fruit	♐︎	
7 Wed	1ʰ Rt 2-5ʰ	♐︎♑︎ 2ʰ	**Pg** 18ʰ
8 Thu	Root from 7ʰ to 23ʰ	♑︎	
9 Fri	Flower from 0ʰ	♒︎ 0ʰ	
10 Sat	Flower to 16ʰ / Leaf from 17ʰ	♒︎♓︎ 17ʰ	◯ 10ʰ
11 Sun	Leaf to 6ʰ / Fruit 7ʰ to 16ʰ / Leaf from 17ʰ	♓︎	▲
12 Mon	Leaf	♓︎	
13 Tue	Leaf to 10ʰ / Fruit from 11ʰ	♓︎♈︎ 11ʰ	
14 Wed	Fruit to 10ʰ	♈︎	☊ 15ʰ
15 Thu	Fr 2ʰ - 7ʰ / Root from 8ʰ	♈︎♉︎ 8ʰ	⚫

Northern Transplanting Time (N T T) — 1 Thu to 3 Sat

Southern Transplanting Time — 4 Sun to 15 Thu

In UK/Ireland remember to add 1 hour for Daylight Saving Time

---

Transplanting Time
(time of descending Moon in northern hemisphere)
Aug 22 to Sep 5 12ʰ and Sep 19 0ʰ to Oct 2

Leaf times

- Tend leafy plants (like lettuce) during these times.

Root times

- Tend root plants (carrots, potatoes) during these times.
- The harvest of **root crops** is always best undertaken at Root times. Storage trials of onions, carrots, beetroots (beets) and potatoes have demonstrated this time and again.

Fruit times

- Tend fruit plants (beans, grains, tomatoes) during these times.
- Good times to **harvest fruit** are when the Moon is in Sagittarius or Aries (Sep 5 0ʰ to Sep 7 1ʰ, and Sep 13 11ʰ to Sep 15 7ʰ), or other Fruit times, always avoiding unfavourable times.
- Good times for **sowing winter grain** are when the Moon is in Leo or Sagittarius (Sep 5 0ʰ to Sep 7 1ʰ, and Sep 22 to Sep 25) avoiding unfavourable times, and at other Fruit times.
- **Rye** can, if necessary, also be sown at Root times with all subsequent cultivations being carried out at Fruit times.

Flower times

- Tend flowering plants (broccoli, roses) during these times.
- During Transplanting Time transplant annuals and bienniels that were sown earlier.

Date	My notes	Planetary aspects (**Bold** = visible to naked eye)

Planet positions in zodiac

☿	Mercury	♍	(10 R)
♀	Venus	♌	
♂	Mars	♉	
♃	Jupiter	♓	(R)
♄	Saturn	♑	(R)
♅	Uranus	♈	(R)
♆	Neptune	♓	(R)
♇	Pluto	♐	(R)

1
2 ☽ ☍ ♁ 3ʰ
3 ☿ ☌ ♃ 2ʰ ☽ ☍ ♂ 12ʰ

4
5
6 ☽ ☌ ♇ 22ʰ
7
8 **☽ ☌ ♄ 13ʰ**
9 ☽ ☍ ♀ 14ʰ
10 **☾ ☌ ♆ 21ʰ**

11 ☉ △ ♁ 13ʰ **☾ ☌ ♃ 17ʰ** **☾ ☍ ☿ 22ʰ**
12
13
14 **☾ ☌ ♁ 23ʰ**
15

Planet (naked eye) visibility

Evening:
–

All night:
Mars, Jupiter, Saturn

Morning:
Venus

♓	Pisces	♈	Aries	♉	Taurus	♊	Gemini	♋	Cancer	♌	Leo
♍	Virgo	♎	Libra	♏	Scorpio	♐	Sagittarius	♑	Capricorn	♒	Aquarius

NB: All zodiac symbols refer to astronomical constellations, not astrological signs (see p. 10)

Control pests
(see p. 74 for details)

- **Flies:** burn fly papers at Flower times.

Southern hemisphere

Southern Transplanting Time
Sep 5 16ʰ to Sep 18 20ʰ

Biodynamic preparations

Cut **yarrow** in the mornings at Fruit times before Sep 15. The blossoms should show some seed formation.

My notes

My notes

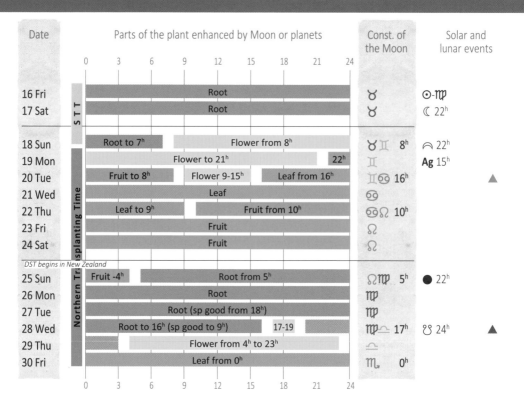

Date	Parts of the plant enhanced by Moon or planets	Const. of the Moon	Solar and lunar events
16 Fri	Root	♉	☉-♍
17 Sat	Root	♉	☾ 22ʰ
18 Sun	Root to 7ʰ / Flower from 8ʰ	♉♊ 8ʰ	⚊ 22ʰ
19 Mon	Flower to 21ʰ / 22ʰ	♊	Ag 15ʰ
20 Tue	Fruit to 8ʰ / Flower 9-15ʰ / Leaf from 16ʰ	♊♋ 16ʰ	
21 Wed	Leaf	♋	▲
22 Thu	Leaf to 9ʰ / Fruit from 10ʰ	♋♌ 10ʰ	
23 Fri	Fruit	♌	
24 Sat	Fruit	♌	
25 Sun	Fruit -4ʰ / Root from 5ʰ	♌♍ 5ʰ	● 22ʰ
26 Mon	Root	♍	
27 Tue	Root (sp good from 18ʰ)	♍	
28 Wed	Root to 16ʰ (sp good to 9ʰ) / 17-19	♍♎ 17ʰ	☍ 24ʰ
29 Thu	Flower from 4ʰ to 23ʰ	♎	▲
30 Fri	Leaf from 0ʰ	♏ 0ʰ	

STT

Northern Transplanting Time

DST begins in New Zealand

In UK/Ireland remember to add 1 hour for Daylight Saving Time

---

Transplanting Time
(time of descending Moon in northern hemisphere)
Sep 19 0ʰ to Oct 2

Leaf times

- Tend leafy plants (like lettuce) during these times.
- Plant conifer and evergreen shrubs.

Root times

- Tend root plants (carrots, potatoes) during these times.
- The harvest of **root crops** is always best undertaken at Root times. Storage trials of onions, carrots, beetroots (beets) and potatoes have demonstrated this time and again.
- Sow radishes in a cold frame.

Fruit times

- Tend fruit plants (beans, grains, tomatoes) during these times.
- Good times to **harvest fruit** are when the Moon is in Sagittarius or Aries, or other Fruit times (Sep 22 10ʰ to Sep 25 4ʰ) always avoiding unfavourable times.
- Good times for **sowing winter grain** are when the Moon is in Leo or Sagittarius (Sep 5 to 7, and Sep 22 10ʰ to Sep 25 4ʰ).
- **Rye** can if necessary also be sown at Root times with all subsequent cultivations being carried out at Fruit times.

Flower times

- Tend flowering plants (broccoli, roses) during these times.
- During Transplanting Time transplant annuals and bienniels sown earlier.

Date	My notes	Planetary aspects
		(**Bold** = visible to naked eye)

Date	Aspects
16	☉☍♆ 22ʰ
17	☾☌♂ 1ʰ
18	☿☍♃ 23ʰ
19	☉△♇ 4ʰ
20	♀△♅ 5ʰ ☾☍♇ 13ʰ
21	
22	☾☍♄ 11ʰ
23	☉☌☿ 7ʰ
24	♀☍♆ 9ʰ
25	☾☍♆ 5ʰ ☾☌♀ 7ʰ ☾☌☿ 13ʰ
26	☽☍♃ 0ʰ ♀△♇ 6ʰ ☿☌♀ 18ʰ ☉☍♃ 19ʰ
27	☿△♇ 13ʰ
28	♂△♄ 6ʰ
29	☽☍♅ 8ʰ
30	

Planet positions in zodiac

☿	Mercury	♍	(R)
♀	Venus	♌	24 ♍
♂	Mars	♉	
♃	Jupiter	♓	(R)
♄	Saturn	♑	(R)
♅	Uranus	♈	(R)
♆	Neptune	♓	(R)
♇	Pluto	♐	(R)

Planet (naked eye) visibility

Evening: –

All night:
  Mars, Jupiter, Saturn

Morning:
  Mercury (from Sep 30), Venus

♓ Pisces	♈ Aries	♉ Taurus	♊ Gemini	♋ Cancer	♌ Leo
♍ Virgo	♎ Libra	♏ Scorpio	♐ Sagittarius	♑ Capricorn	♒ Aquarius

NB: All zodiac symbols refer to astronomical constellations, not astrological signs (see p. 10)

Control pests
(see p. 74 for details)

- **Flies:** burn fly papers at Flower times.
- **Slugs:** ash between Sep 20 16ʰ and Sep 22 19ʰ.

Southern hemisphere

Southern Transplanting Time
Sep 5 to Sep 18 20ʰ

Maria Thun's tree log preparations

- Cut **maple** logs, fill with dried **dandelion** and put them into the ground between Sep 16 11ʰ and Sep 17 4ʰ.
- Cut **larch** logs, fill with dried **camomile** and put them into the ground between Sep 18 12ʰ and Sep 19 5ʰ.
- Cut **birch** logs, fill with dried **yarrow** and put them into the ground between Sep 23 22ʰ and Sep 24 15ʰ.

My notes

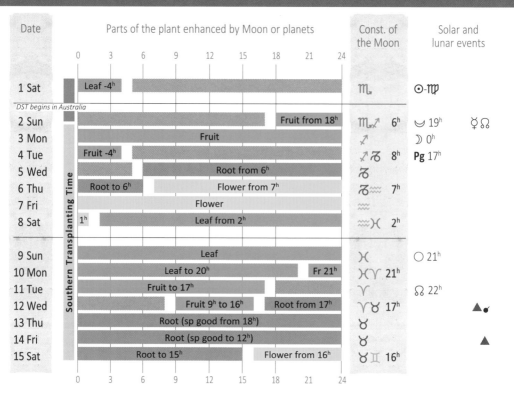

Date	Parts of the plant enhanced by Moon or planets	Const. of the Moon	Solar and lunar events
1 Sat	Leaf -4ʰ	♏	☉-♍
DST begins in Australia			
2 Sun	Fruit from 18ʰ	♏♐ 6ʰ	☽ 19ʰ ☿ ☊
3 Mon	Fruit	♐	☽ 0ʰ
4 Tue	Fruit -4ʰ	♐♑ 8ʰ	**Pg** 17ʰ
5 Wed	Root from 6ʰ	♑	
6 Thu	Root to 6ʰ / Flower from 7ʰ	♑♒ 7ʰ	
7 Fri	Flower	♒	
8 Sat	1ʰ / Leaf from 2ʰ	♒♓ 2ʰ	
9 Sun	Leaf	♓	○ 21ʰ
10 Mon	Leaf to 20ʰ / Fr 21ʰ	♓♈ 21ʰ	
11 Tue	Fruit to 17ʰ	♈	☊ 22ʰ
12 Wed	Fruit 9ʰ to 16ʰ / Root from 17ʰ	♈♉ 17ʰ	▲ ☌
13 Thu	Root (sp good from 18ʰ)	♉	
14 Fri	Root (sp good to 12ʰ)	♉	▲
15 Sat	Root to 15ʰ / Flower from 16ʰ	♉♊ 16ʰ	

Southern Transplanting Time

In UK/Ireland remember to add 1 hour for Daylight Saving Time

---

Transplanting Time
(time of descending Moon in northern hemisphere)
Sep 19 to Oct 2 17ʰ and Oct 16 8ʰ to Oct 29 23ʰ

Fruit times

- Tend fruit plants (beans, grains, tomatoes) during these times.
- **Store fruit** at any Fruit or Flower time outside Transplanting Time.
- Harvest any ripe fruit.

Leaf times

- Tend leafy plants (like lettuce) during these times.
- Harvest **seeds of leaf plants.**
- Sow spinach, winter lettuce, lamb's lettuce (in a greenhouse if necessary).

Flower times

- Tend flowering plants (broccoli, roses) during these times.
- Harvest **seeds of flower plants.**
- Sow annual sweet peas in a greenhouse.

Root times

- Tend root plants (carrots, potatoes) during these times.
- Harvest **seeds of root plants.**
- In sunny regions sow radishes.

Date	My notes	Planetary aspects
		(**Bold** = visible to naked eye)

Date	Planetary aspects
1	☽ ☍ ♂ 15ʰ ♀ ☍ ♃ 18ʰ
2	☿ ☊ 5ʰ
3	
4	☽ ☌ ♇ 4ʰ
5	☽ ☌ ♄ 18ʰ
6	
7	☿ △ ♇ 4ʰ
8	☽ ☌ ♆ 5ʰ ☽ ☍ ☿ 11ʰ ☽ ☌ ♃ 20ʰ
9	☽ ☍ ♀ 14ʰ
10	
11	
12	☉ △ ♄ 1ʰ ☾ ● ☊ 6ʰ ☿ ☍ ♃ 7ʰ
13	
14	♀ △ ♄ 6ʰ
15	☾ ☌ ♂ 4ʰ

Planet positions in zodiac

☿	Mercury	♍ (R 2 D)
♀	Venus	♍
♂	Mars	♉
♃	Jupiter	♓ (R)
♄	Saturn	♑ (R)
⛢	Uranus	♈ (R)
♆	Neptune	♓ (R)
♇	Pluto	♐ (R 8 D)

Planet (naked eye) visibility

Evening:
Saturn

All night:
Mars, Jupiter

Morning:
Mercury, Venus (to Oct 2)

♓ Pisces	♈ Aries	♉ Taurus	♊ Gemini	♋ Cancer	♌ Leo
♍ Virgo	♎ Libra	♏ Scorpio	♐ Sagittarius	♑ Capricorn	♒ Aquarius

NB: All zodiac symbols refer to astronomical constellations, not astrological signs (see p. 10)

Control pests
(see p. 74 for details)
- **Flies:** burn fly papers at Flower times.

Southern hemisphere
Southern Transplanting Time
Oct 2 21ʰ to Oct 16 4ʰ and Oct 30 3ʰ to Nov 12

Treating cleared ground
All **cleared ground** should be treated with compost and sprayed with barrel preparation, and ploughed ready for winter.

My notes

My notes

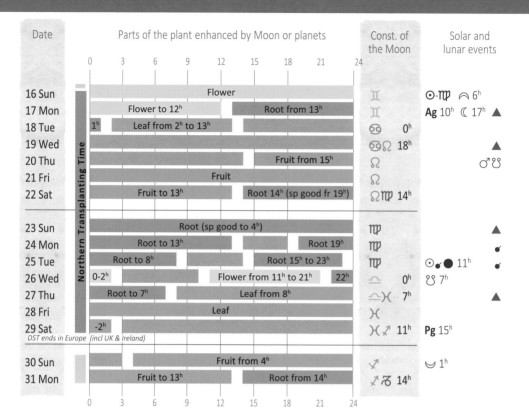

Date	Parts of the plant enhanced by Moon or planets	Const. of the Moon	Solar and lunar events
16 Sun	Flower	♊	☉-♍ ⌒ 6ʰ
17 Mon	Flower to 12ʰ — Root from 13ʰ	♊	**Ag** 10ʰ ☾ 17ʰ ▲
18 Tue	1ʰ — Leaf from 2ʰ to 13ʰ	♋ 0ʰ	
19 Wed		♋♌ 18ʰ	▲
20 Thu	Fruit from 15ʰ	♌	♂☊
21 Fri	Fruit	♌	
22 Sat	Fruit to 13ʰ — Root 14ʰ (sp good fr 19ʰ)	♌♍ 14ʰ	
23 Sun	Root (sp good to 4ʰ)	♍	▲
24 Mon	Root to 13ʰ — Root 19ʰ	♍	
25 Tue	Root to 8ʰ — Root 15ʰ to 23ʰ	♍	☉⚳● 11ʰ ⚳
26 Wed	0-2ʰ — Flower from 11ʰ to 21ʰ — 22ʰ	♎ 0ʰ	☊ 7ʰ
27 Thu	Root to 7ʰ — Leaf from 8ʰ	♎♓ 7ʰ	▲
28 Fri	Leaf	♓	
29 Sat	-2ʰ	♓♐ 11ʰ	**Pg** 15ʰ
DST ends in Europe (incl UK & Ireland)			
30 Sun	Fruit from 4ʰ	♐	⌣ 1ʰ
31 Mon	Fruit to 13ʰ — Root from 14ʰ	♐♑ 14ʰ	

Northern Transplanting Time

In UK/Ireland remember to add 1 hour for Daylight Saving Time

Transplanting Time
(time of descending Moon in northern hemisphere)
Oct 16 8ʰ to Oct 29 23ʰ

Leaf times

- Tend leafy plants (like lettuce) during these times.
- Harvest **seeds of leaf plants.**
- Transplant conifer and evergreen shrubs.
- Transplant cabbage.

Root times

- Tend root plants (carrots, potatoes) during these times.
- Harvest **seeds of root plants.**
- Sow carrots, transplant onions.

Fruit times

- Tend fruit plants (beans, grains, tomatoes) during these times.
- **Store fruit** at any Fruit or Flower time outside Transplanting Time.
- Transplant strawberries.

Flower times

- Tend flowering plants (broccoli, roses) during these times.
- Harvest **seeds of flower plants.**
- Plant hyacinths, tulips and lilies.
- Transplant bienniels.

Treating cleared ground
All **cleared ground** should be treated with compost and sprayed with barrel preparation, and ploughed ready for winter.

Date	My notes	Planetary aspects (**Bold** = visible to naked eye)

Planet positions in zodiac

☿ Mercury ♍︎
♀ Venus ♍︎ 31 ♎︎
♂ Mars ♉︎ (30 R)
♃ Jupiter ♓︎ (R)
♄ Saturn ♑︎ (R 23 D)
⛢ Uranus ♈︎ (R)
♆ Neptune ♓︎ (R)
♇ Pluto ♐︎

Date	Planetary aspects
16	
17	☾ ☍ ♇ 21ʰ ☉ △ ♂ 22ʰ
18	
19	♀ △ ♂ 2ʰ ☾ ☍ ♄ 18ʰ
20	♂ ☍ ☊ 2ʰ
21	
22	☾ ☍ ♆ 13ʰ ☉ ☌ ♀ 22ʰ
23	☿ △ ♄ 1ʰ ☾ ☍ ♃ 2ʰ
24	**☾ ☌ ☿ 16ʰ**
25	☽ ☌ ♀ 12ʰ
26	☽ ☍ ⛢ 14ʰ
27	☿ △ ♂ 4ʰ
28	
29	☽ ☍ ♂ 6ʰ
30	
31	☽ ☌ ♇ 9ʰ

Planet (naked eye) visibility

Evening:
Saturn

All night:
Mars, Jupiter

Morning:
Mercury (to Oct 26)

♓︎ Pisces	♈︎ Aries	♉︎ Taurus	♊︎ Gemini	♋︎ Cancer	♌︎ Leo
♍︎ Virgo	♎︎ Libra	♏︎ Scorpio	♐︎ Sagittarius	♑︎ Capricorn	♒︎ Aquarius

Control pests
(see p. 74 for details)

- **Flies:** burn fly papers at Flower times.
- **Slugs:** ash between Oct 18 0ʰ and Oct 19 17ʰ.

Southern hemisphere

Southern Transplanting Time
Oct 2 to Oct 16 4ʰ and Oct 30 3ʰ to Nov 12

My notes

My notes

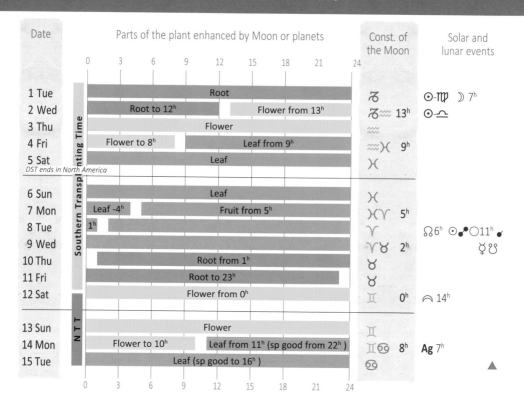

Date	Parts of the plant enhanced by Moon or planets	Const. of the Moon	Solar and lunar events
1 Tue	Root	♑	☉–♍ ☽ 7ʰ
2 Wed	Root to 12ʰ / Flower from 13ʰ	♑ ♒ 13ʰ	☉–♎
3 Thu	Flower	♒	
4 Fri	Flower to 8ʰ / Leaf from 9ʰ	♒ ♓ 9ʰ	
5 Sat	Leaf	♓	
DST ends in North America			
6 Sun	Leaf	♓	
7 Mon	Leaf -4ʰ / Fruit from 5ʰ	♓ ♈ 5ʰ	
8 Tue	1ʰ	♈	☽♈6ʰ ☉ ⚡ ○11ʰ ♐
9 Wed		♈ ♉ 2ʰ	☿ ♋
10 Thu	Root from 1ʰ	♉	
11 Fri	Root to 23ʰ	♉	
12 Sat	Flower from 0ʰ	♊ 0ʰ	⚹ 14ʰ
13 Sun	Flower	♊	
14 Mon	Flower to 10ʰ / Leaf from 11ʰ (sp good from 22ʰ)	♊ ♋ 8ʰ	**Ag** 7ʰ
15 Tue	Leaf (sp good to 16ʰ)	♋	▲

(left vertical label: *Southern Transplanting Time* ; *N T T*)

Transplanting Time
(time of descending Moon in northern hemisphere)
Nov 12 16ʰ to Nov 26 7ʰ

Leaf times

- Tend leafy plants (like lettuce) during these times.
- Transplant hedges and climbing shrubs during Transplanting Time.

Root times

- Tend root plants (carrots, potatoes) during these times.
- Harvest Jerusalem artichokes, parsnips, leeks.

Fruit times

- Tend fruit plants (beans, grains, tomatoes) during these times.
- **Fruit and forest trees** will benefit from a spraying of horn manure and/or barrel preparation when being transplanted at Fruit times.
- In warm regions harvest table olives.

Flower times

- Tend flowering plants (broccoli, roses) during these times.
- Cut **Advent greenery** and **Christmas trees** for transporting.
- Plant wisterias, begonias and clematis.
- Cut back rose shrubs.
- Sow sweet peas for germinating next spring.

Date	My notes	Planetary aspects (**Bold** = visible to naked eye)
1		**☽☌♄ 23^{h}**
2		
3		
4		☽☌♆ 11^{h} **☽☌♃ 22^{h}**
5		♀☍♅ 22^{h}
6		
7		
8		☽☍☿ 11^{h} ☾●♅ 13^{h} ☉☌☿ 17^{h} ☾☍♀ 20^{h}
9		☿☍♅ 3^{h} ☉☍♅ 8^{h} ☿☋ 12^{h}
10		♀△♆ 12^{h}
11		**☾☌♂ 14^{h}**
12		☿△♆ 19^{h}
13		
14		☾☍♇ 6^{h}
15		☉△♆ 4^{h} ♀△♃ 10^{h}

Planet positions in zodiac

☿ Mercury	♍ 4 ♎ 15 ♏	
♀ Venus	♎ 14 ♏	
♂ Mars	♉	(R)
♃ Jupiter	♓	(R)
♄ Saturn	♑	
♅ Uranus	♈	(R)
♆ Neptune	♓	(R)
♇ Pluto	♐	

Planet (naked eye) visibility

Evening:
Saturn

All night:
Mars, Jupiter

Morning:
–

♓ Pisces ♈ Aries ♉ Taurus ♊ Gemini ♋ Cancer ♌ Leo
♍ Virgo ♎ Libra ♏ Scorpio ♐ Sagittarius ♑ Capricorn ♒ Aquarius

NB: All zodiac symbols refer to astronomical constellations, not astrological signs (see p. 10)

Control pests
(see p. 74 for details)

- **Flies:** burn fly papers at Flower times.

Southern hemisphere

Southern Transplanting Time
Oct 30 to Nov 12 12^{h} and Nov 26 11^{h} to Dec 9

Maria Thun's tree log preparations

- Cut **birch** logs, fill with dried **yarrow** and put them into the ground between Nov 5 11^{h} and Nov 6 4^{h}.

My notes

Compost

If not already completed in October, all organic waste materials should be gathered and made into a **compost.** Applying the biodynamic preparations to the compost will ensure a rapid transformation and good fungal development. An application of barrel preparation will also help the composting process.

Date	Parts of the plant enhanced by Moon or planets	Const. of the Moon	Solar and lunar events

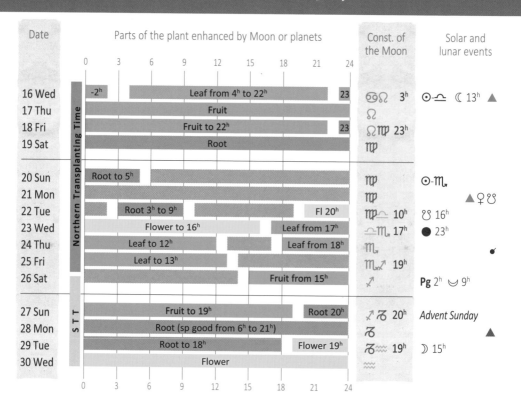

Chart contents (times 0–24):

Northern Transplanting Time

- 16 Wed — -2ʰ | Leaf from 4ʰ to 22ʰ | 23 — ♋♌ 3ʰ — ☉♎ ☽ 13ʰ ▲
- 17 Thu — Fruit — ♌
- 18 Fri — Fruit to 22ʰ | 23 — ♌♍ 23ʰ
- 19 Sat — Root — ♍

- 20 Sun — Root to 5ʰ — ♍ — ☉-♏
- 21 Mon — ♍ — ▲♀☯
- 22 Tue — Root 3ʰ to 9ʰ | Fl 20ʰ — ♍♎ 10ʰ — ☯ 16ʰ
- 23 Wed — Flower to 16ʰ | Leaf from 17ʰ — ♎♏ 17ʰ — ● 23ʰ
- 24 Thu — Leaf to 12ʰ | Leaf from 18ʰ — ♏
- 25 Fri — Leaf to 13ʰ — ♏♐ 19ʰ
- 26 Sat — Fruit from 15ʰ — ♐ — Pg 2ʰ ☋ 9ʰ

S T T

- 27 Sun — Fruit to 19ʰ | Root 20ʰ — ♐♑ 20ʰ — *Advent Sunday*
- 28 Mon — Root (sp good from 6ʰ to 21ʰ) — ♑ — ▲
- 29 Tue — Root to 18ʰ | Flower 19ʰ — ♑♒ 19ʰ — ☽ 15ʰ
- 30 Wed — Flower — ♒

Transplanting Time
(time of descending Moon in northern hemisphere)
Nov 12 to Nov 26 7ʰ

Leaf times

- Tend leafy plants (like lettuce) during these times.
- Harvest Brussels sprouts, lettuce, spinach.
- Transplant hedges and climbing shrubs during Transplanting Time.

Root times

- Tend root plants (carrots, potatoes) during these times.

Fruit times

- Tend fruit plants (beans, grains, tomatoes) during these times.
- **Fruit and forest trees** will benefit from a spraying of horn manure and/or barrel preparation when being transplanted at Fruit times.
- Prune fruit trees and shrubs.

Flower times

- Tend flowering plants (broccoli, roses) during these times.
- Cut **Advent greenery** and **Christmas trees** for transporting.

Date	My notes	Planetary aspects (**Bold** = visible to naked eye)
16		☾☌♄ 3ʰ ☿△♃ 16ʰ
17		
18		☾☍♆ 21ʰ
19		☾☍♃ 9ʰ
20		
21		☉△♃ 4ʰ ♀♋ 14ʰ ☿☌♀ 23ʰ
22		☾☍♅ 21ʰ
23		
24		☽☌♀ 13ʰ ☽●☿ 15ʰ
25		☽☍♂ 7ʰ
26		
27		☽☌♇ 17ʰ
28		♂△♄ 18ʰ
29		☽☌♄ 7ʰ ☿☍♂ 21ʰ
30		

Planet positions in zodiac

☿ Mercury	♏
♀ Venus	♏
♂ Mars	♉ (R)
♃ Jupiter	♓ (R 23 D)
♄ Saturn	♑
♅ Uranus	♈ (R)
♆ Neptune	♓ (R)
♇ Pluto	♐

Planet (naked eye) visibility

Evening:
Saturn

All night:
Mars, Jupiter

Morning:
–

| ♓ Pisces | ♈ Aries | ♉ Taurus | ♊ Gemini | ♋ Cancer | ♌ Leo |
| ♍ Virgo | ♎ Libra | ♏ Scorpio | ♐ Sagittarius | ♑ Capricorn | ♒ Aquarius |

NB: All zodiac symbols refer to astronomical constellations, not astrological signs (see p. 10)

Control pests
(see p. 74 for details)

- **Flies:** burn fly papers at Flower times.

Southern hemisphere

Southern Transplanting Time
Nov 26 11ʰ to Dec 9

Maria Thun's tree log preparations

- Cut **larch** logs, fill with dried **camomile** and put them into the ground between Nov 29 10ʰ and Nov 30 3ʰ.

Compost

If not already completed in October, all organic waste materials should be gathered and made into a **compost.** Applying the biodynamic preparations to the compost will ensure a rapid transformation and good fungal development. An application of barrel preparation will also help the composting process.

My notes

Date	Parts of the plant enhanced by Moon or planets	Const. of the Moon	Solar and lunar events
1 Thu	Flower to 13ʰ / Leaf from 14ʰ	♒︎♓︎ 14ʰ	☉-♏︎
2 Fri	Leaf	♓︎	
3 Sat	Leaf	♓︎	
4 Sun	Leaf to 10ʰ / Fruit from 11ʰ	♓︎♈︎ 11ʰ	
5 Mon	Fruit to 8ʰ / Fr 21ʰ	♈︎	☊ 13ʰ
6 Tue	Fruit to 8ʰ / Root from 9ʰ	♈︎♉︎ 9ʰ	
7 Wed	Root	♉︎	
8 Thu	1ʰ / Root from 7ʰ	♉︎	○ 4ʰ
9 Fri	Root to 6ʰ / Flower from 7ʰ	♉︎♊︎ 7ʰ	⌒ 21ʰ
10 Sat	Flower	♊︎	
11 Sun	Flower	♊︎♋︎ 16ʰ	
12 Mon	Fl to 4ʰ / Leaf from 5ʰ	♋︎	**Ag** 1ʰ
13 Tue	Leaf to 9ʰ / Fruit from 10ʰ	♋︎♌︎ 10ʰ	
14 Wed	Fruit	♌︎	
15 Thu	Fruit	♌︎	

Southern Transplanting Time (Dec 1 – Dec 9)

NTT (Dec 11 – Dec 15)

Transplanting Time
(time of descending Moon in northern hemisphere)
Dec 9 23ʰ to Dec 23 16ʰ

Fruit times
- Tend fruit plants (beans, grains, tomatoes) during these times.

Leaf times
- Tend leafy plants (like lettuce) during these times.
- On a mild day, prune deciduous trees during Transplanting Time.

Flower times
- Tend flowering plants (broccoli, roses) during these times.
- Cut **Advent greenery** and **Christmas trees** to ensure lasting fragrance.

Root times
- Tend root plants (carrots, potatoes) during these times.

Pruning trees and hedges
- Transplanting Time is good for **pruning trees and hedges.** Fruit trees should be pruned at Fruit or Flower times.

Date	My notes	Planetary aspects (**Bold** = visible to naked eye)

Planet positions in zodiac

☿ Mercury	♏ 6 ♐
♀ Venus	♏ 9 ♐
♂ Mars	♉ (R)
♃ Jupiter	♓
♄ Saturn	♑
⛢ Uranus	♈ (R)
♆ Neptune	♓ (R 4 D)
♇ Pluto	♐

Date	Aspects
1	♀☍♂ 5ʰ ☽☌♆ 16ʰ
2	☽☌♃ 3ʰ
3	
4	
5	☽•⛢ 18ʰ
6	
7	
8	☽•♂ 4ʰ ☉☍♂ 6ʰ
9	☾☍♀ 5ʰ ☾☍☿ 16ʰ
10	
11	☾☍♇ 14ʰ
12	
13	☾☍♄ 14ʰ
14	
15	

Planet (naked eye) visibility

Evening:
Mercury (from Dec 14),
Venus (from Dec 3), Saturn

All night:
Mars, Jupiter

Morning:
—

| ♓ Pisces | ♈ Aries | ♉ Taurus | ♊ Gemini | ♋ Cancer | ♌ Leo |
| ♍ Virgo | ♎ Libra | ♏ Scorpio | ♐ Sagittarius | ♑ Capricorn | ♒ Aquarius |

NB: All zodiac symbols refer to astronomical constellations, not astrological signs (see p. 10)

Control pests
(see p. 74 for details)

- Burn feathers or skins of **warm blooded pests** from Dec 6 9ʰ to Dec 9 1ʰ. *The burning (and grinding) should be completed by Dec 9 1ʰ.*

My notes

Southern hemisphere

Southern Transplanting Time
Nov 26 to Dec 9 19ʰ and Dec 23 20ʰ to Jan 6

Harvest time for seeds (always avoiding unfavourable times):
- *Leaf seeds:* Leaf times.
- *Fruit seeds:* Fruit times, preferably with Moon in Leo (Dec 13 10ʰ to Dec 16 7ʰ).
- *Root seeds:* At Root times.
- *Flower seeds:* Dec 9 7ʰ to Dec 11 15ʰ, and at other Flower times.
- *Control slugs:* Dec 11 16ʰ to Dec 13 9ʰ.

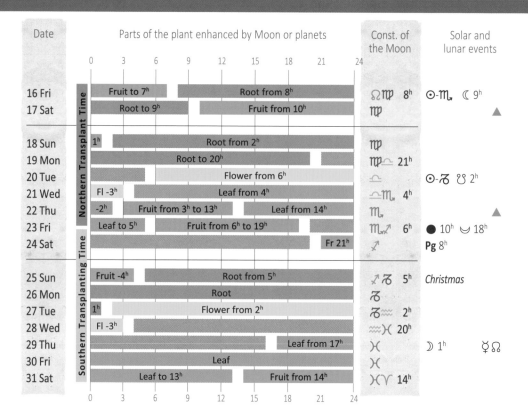

Date	Parts of the plant enhanced by Moon or planets	Const. of the Moon	Solar and lunar events
16 Fri	Fruit to 7ʰ / Root from 8ʰ	♌︎♍︎ 8ʰ	☉-♏︎ ☽ 9ʰ
17 Sat	Root to 9ʰ / Fruit from 10ʰ	♍︎	▲
18 Sun	1ʰ / Root from 2ʰ	♍︎	
19 Mon	Root to 20ʰ	♍︎♎︎ 21ʰ	
20 Tue	Flower from 6ʰ	♎︎	☉-♐︎ ☊ 2ʰ
21 Wed	Fl -3ʰ / Leaf from 4ʰ	♎︎♏︎ 4ʰ	
22 Thu	-2ʰ / Fruit from 3ʰ to 13ʰ / Leaf from 14ʰ	♏︎	▲
23 Fri	Leaf to 5ʰ / Fruit from 6ʰ to 19ʰ	♏︎♐︎ 6ʰ	● 10ʰ ☋ 18ʰ
24 Sat	Fr 21ʰ	♐︎	Pg 8ʰ
25 Sun	Fruit -4ʰ / Root from 5ʰ	♐︎♑︎ 5ʰ	*Christmas*
26 Mon	Root	♑︎	
27 Tue	1ʰ / Flower from 2ʰ	♑︎♒︎ 2ʰ	
28 Wed	Fl -3ʰ	♒︎♓︎ 20ʰ	
29 Thu	Leaf from 17ʰ	♓︎	☽ 1ʰ ☿ ♌︎
30 Fri	Leaf	♓︎	
31 Sat	Leaf to 13ʰ / Fruit from 14ʰ	♓︎♈︎ 14ʰ	

Northern Transplant Time (16–23)
Southern Transplanting Time (24–31)

Transplanting Time
(time of descending Moon in northern hemisphere)
Dec 9 to Dec 23 16ʰ

Fruit times
- Tend fruit plants (beans, grains, tomatoes) during these times.

Leaf times
- Tend leafy plants (like lettuce) during these times.

Flower times
- Tend flowering plants (broccoli, roses) during these times.
- Cut **Advent greenery** and **Christmas trees** to ensure lasting fragrance.

Root times
- Tend root plants (carrots, potatoes) during these times.

Pruning trees and hedges
- Transplanting Time is good for **pruning trees and hedges.** Fruit trees should be pruned at Fruit or Flower times.

Date	My notes	Planetary aspects (**Bold** = visible to naked eye)
16		☾☍♆ 6^h ☾☍♃ 19^h
17		☿△⛢ 22^h
18		
19		
20		☾☍⛢ 7^h
21		
22		☾☍♂ 2^h ♀△⛢ 10^h
23		
24		**☽☌♀ 12^h ☽☌☿ 20^h**
25		☽☌♇ 3^h
26		**☽☌♄ 18^h**
27		
28		☽☌♆ 22^h
29		☿☊ 4^h **☽☌♃ 12^h ☿☌♀ 14^h**
30		
31		

Planet positions in zodiac

☿ Mercury	♐	(29 R)
♀ Venus	♐	
♂ Mars	♉	(R)
♃ Jupiter	♓	
♄ Saturn	♑	
⛢ Uranus	♈	(R)
♆ Neptune	♓	
♇ Pluto	♐	

Planet (naked eye) visibility

Evening:
Mercury (to Dec 30), Venus, Jupiter, Saturn

All night:
Mars

Morning:
–

♓ Pisces ♈ Aries ♉ Taurus ♊ Gemini ♋ Cancer ♌ Leo
♍ Virgo ♎ Libra ♏ Scorpio ♐ Sagittarius ♑ Capricorn ♒ Aquarius

My notes

Southern hemisphere

Southern Transplanting Time
Dec 23 20^h to Jan 6

Harvest time for seeds (always avoiding unfavourable times):

- ***Leaf seeds:*** Leaf times.
- ***Fruit seeds:*** Fruit times, preferably with Moon in Leo (Dec 13 10^h to Dec 16 7^h).
- ***Root seeds:*** Dec 16 8^h to Dec 17 9^h, Dec 18 2^h to Dec 19 20^h, and at other Root times.
- ***Flower seeds:*** Dec 27 2^h to Dec 28 3^h, and at other Flower times.

Crop tables

Following tables suggest suitable times for sowing and harvesting particular crops. This makes it easier to find the right calendar page for detailed timings. The times are for northern hemisphere, and may need adjusting to your local climate. Between these times, the plants need tending: thinning out, transplanting, hoeing, weeding, watering, composting or manuring.

- Sow and plant in the greenhouse or under cover, depending on the season and your local climate.
- Transplant during Transplanting Time (descending Moon) at Root, Leaf, Flower or Fruit time as appropriate.
- Tend (hoeing, weeding, watering, composting) and harvest at Root, Leaf, Flower or Fruit time as appropriate.

Root vegetables

Beets

Sow	Jan	Feb	Mar	April	May	June	July	Aug	Sep	Oct	Nov	Dec
Harvest	Jan	Feb	Mar	April	May	June	July	Aug	Sep	Oct	Nov	Dec

Carrots

Sow	Jan	Feb	Mar	April	May	June	July	Aug	Sep	Oct	Nov	Dec
Harvest	Jan	Feb	Mar	April	May	June	July	Aug	Sep	Oct	Nov	Dec

Celeriac

Sow	Jan	Feb	Mar	April	May	June	July	Aug	Sep	Oct	Nov	Dec
Harvest	Jan	Feb	Mar	April	May	June	July	Aug	Sep	Oct	Nov	Dec

Garlic

Sow	Jan	Feb	Mar	April	May	June	July	Aug	Sep	Oct	Nov	Dec
Harvest	Jan	Feb	Mar	April	May	June	July	Aug	Sep	Oct	Nov	Dec

Horseradish

Sow	Jan	Feb	Mar	April	May	June	July	Aug	Sep	Oct	Nov	Dec
Harvest	Jan	Feb	Mar	April	May	June	July	Aug	Sep	Oct	Nov	Dec

Jerusalem artichoke

Sow	Jan	Feb	Mar	April	May	June	July	Aug	Sep	Oct	Nov	Dec
Harvest	Jan	Feb	Mar	April	May	June	July	Aug	Sep	Oct	Nov	Dec

Onion

Sow	Jan	Feb	Mar	April	May	June	July	Aug	Sep	Oct	Nov	Dec
Harvest	Jan	Feb	Mar	April	May	June	July	Aug	Sep	Oct	Nov	Dec

Parsnip

	Jan	Feb	Mar	April	May	June	July	Aug	Sep	Oct	Nov	Dec
Sow	Jan	**Feb**	**Mar**	**April**	**May**	**June**	July	Aug	Sep	Oct	Nov	Dec
Harvest	**Jan**	**Feb**	**Mar**	**April**	May	June	July	Aug	**Sep**	**Oct**	**Nov**	**Dec**

Potato, root tubers

	Jan	Feb	Mar	April	May	June	July	Aug	Sep	Oct	Nov	Dec
Sow	Jan	**Feb**	**Mar**	**April**	May	June	July	Aug	Sep	Oct	Nov	Dec
Harvest	Jan	Feb	Mar	**April**	**May**	**June**	**July**	**Aug**	**Sep**	Oct	Nov	Dec

Radish

	Jan	Feb	Mar	April	May	June	July	Aug	Sep	Oct	Nov	Dec
Sow	**Jan**	**Feb**	**Mar**	**April**	**May**	**June**	**July**	**Aug**	**Sep**	**Oct**	**Nov**	**Dec**
Harvest	**Jan**	**Feb**	**Mar**	**April**	**May**	**June**	**July**	**Aug**	**Sep**	**Oct**	**Nov**	**Dec**

Salsify

	Jan	Feb	Mar	April	May	June	July	Aug	Sep	Oct	Nov	Dec
Sow	Jan	Feb	**Mar**	**April**	**May**	**June**	**July**	**Aug**	Sep	Oct	Nov	Dec
Harvest	**Jan**	**Feb**	Mar	April	May	June	July	Aug	Sep	**Oct**	**Nov**	**Dec**

Shallots

	Jan	Feb	Mar	April	May	June	July	Aug	Sep	Oct	Nov	Dec
Sow	Jan	Feb	Mar	April	May	June	July	Aug	**Sep**	**Oct**	Nov	Dec
Harvest	Jan	**Feb**	**Mar**	April	May	June	July	Aug	Sep	Oct	Nov	Dec

Leaf plants

Asparagus

	Jan	Feb	Mar	April	May	June	July	Aug	Sep	Oct	Nov	Dec
Sow	**Jan**	**Feb**	**Mar**	**April**	**May**	June	July	Aug	Sep	Oct	Nov	Dec
Harvest	Jan	Feb	**Mar**	**April**	**May**	**June**	**July**	**Aug**	**Sep**	Oct	Nov	Dec

Bok choy *see* Chinese cabbage

Brussels sprouts

	Jan	Feb	Mar	April	May	June	July	Aug	Sep	Oct	Nov	Dec
Sow	Jan	Feb	**Mar**	**April**	**May**	June	July	Aug	Sep	Oct	Nov	Dec
Harvest	**Jan**	**Feb**	**Mar**	April	May	June	July	Aug	**Sep**	**Oct**	**Nov**	**Dec**

Cabbage

	Jan	Feb	Mar	April	May	June	July	Aug	Sep	Oct	Nov	Dec
Sow	**Jan**	**Feb**	**Mar**	**April**	**May**	**June**	**July**	**Aug**	**Sep**	**Oct**	Nov	Dec
Harvest	Jan	Feb	Mar	April	**May**	**June**	**July**	**Aug**	**Sep**	**Oct**	**Nov**	**Dec**

Celery

	Jan	Feb	Mar	April	May	June	July	Aug	Sep	Oct	Nov	Dec
Sow	Jan	Feb	**Mar**	**April**	**May**	June	July	Aug	Sep	Oct	Nov	Dec
Harvest	Jan	Feb	Mar	April	May	June	July	**Aug**	**Sep**	**Oct**	**Nov**	**Dec**

Chard

	Jan	Feb	Mar	April	May	June	July	Aug	Sep	Oct	Nov	Dec
Sow	Jan	Feb	Mar	**April**	**May**	**June**	July	Aug	Sep	Oct	Nov	Dec
Harvest	Jan	Feb	Mar	April	May	June	**July**	**Aug**	**Sep**	**Oct**	**Nov**	Dec

Chicory (endives)

	Jan	Feb	Mar	April	May	June	July	Aug	Sep	Oct	Nov	Dec
Sow	Jan	Feb	Mar	April	**May**	**June**	July	Aug	Sep	Oct	Nov	Dec
Harvest	Jan	Feb	Mar	April	May	**June**	**July**	**Aug**	**Sep**	**Oct**	**Nov**	**Dec**

Chinese cabbage (pe-tsai, bok choy)

	Jan	Feb	Mar	April	May	June	July	Aug	Sep	Oct	Nov	Dec
Sow	Jan	Feb	Mar	April	**May**	**June**	**July**	**Aug**	**Sep**	Oct	Nov	Dec
Harvest	Jan	Feb	Mar	April	May	June	July	Aug	**Sep**	**Oct**	**Nov**	**Dec**

Corn salad *see* Lamb's lettuce

Curly kale (green cabbage)

	Jan	Feb	Mar	April	May	June	July	Aug	Sep	Oct	Nov	Dec
Sow	Jan	Feb	Mar	**April**	**May**	**June**	July	Aug	Sep	Oct	Nov	Dec
Harvest	Jan	Feb	Mar	April	May	June	July	Aug	Sep	**Oct**	**Nov**	**Dec**

Endives *see* Chicory

Grass (lawns)

	Jan	Feb	Mar	April	May	June	July	Aug	Sep	Oct	Nov	Dec
Sow	Jan	Feb	Mar	**April**	**May**	June	July	Aug	**Sep**	Oct	Nov	Dec
Mow	Jan	Feb	**Mar**	**April**	**May**	**June**	**July**	**Aug**	**Sep**	**Oct**	Nov	Dec

Green cabbage *see* Curly kale

Kohlrabi

	Jan	Feb	Mar	April	May	June	July	Aug	Sep	Oct	Nov	Dec
Sow	Jan	**Feb**	**Mar**	April	May	June	July	Aug	Sep	Oct	Nov	Dec
Harvest	Jan	Feb	Mar	**April**	**May**	**June**	**July**	**Aug**	**Sep**	**Oct**	**Nov**	**Dec**

Lamb's lettuce (corn salad)

	Jan	Feb	Mar	April	May	June	July	Aug	Sep	Oct	Nov	Dec
Sow	Jan	**Feb**	**Mar**	April	May	June	July	Aug	Sep	Oct	Nov	Dec
Harvest	**Jan**	**Feb**	Mar	April	May	June	July	**Aug**	**Sep**	**Oct**	**Nov**	**Dec**

Leaf herbs

	Jan	Feb	Mar	April	May	June	July	Aug	Sep	Oct	Nov	Dec
Sow	Jan	Feb	**Mar**	**April**	**May**	June	July	Aug	Sep	Oct	Nov	Dec
Harvest	Jan	Feb	Mar	**April**	**May**	**June**	**July**	**Aug**	**Sep**	Oct	Nov	Dec

Leek

	Jan	Feb	Mar	April	May	June	July	Aug	Sep	Oct	Nov	Dec
Sow	**Jan**	**Feb**	**Mar**	April	May	June	July	**Aug**	**Sep**	Oct	Nov	Dec
Harvest	**Jan**	**Feb**	**Mar**	April	May	June	July	Aug	**Sep**	**Oct**	**Nov**	**Dec**

Lettuce, crisphead (iceberg) lettuce

	Jan	Feb	Mar	April	May	June	July	Aug	Sep	Oct	Nov	Dec
Sow	**Jan**	**Feb**	**Mar**	**April**	**May**	**June**	**July**	**Aug**	Sep	Oct	Nov	Dec
Harvest	Jan	**Feb**	**Mar**	**April**	**May**	**June**	**July**	**Aug**	Sep	Oct	**Nov**	Dec

Lettuce, winter

	Jan	Feb	Mar	April	May	June	July	Aug	Sep	Oct	Nov	Dec
Sow	Jan	Feb	Mar	April	May	June	July	**Aug**	**Sep**	**Oct**	Nov	Dec
Harvest	**Jan**	**Feb**	**Mar**	**April**	**May**	June	July	Aug	**Sep**	**Oct**	**Nov**	**Dec**

Red cabbage

	Jan	Feb	Mar	April	May	June	July	Aug	Sep	Oct	Nov	Dec
Sow	Jan	**Feb**	**Mar**	**April**	**May**	**June**	July	Aug	Sep	Oct	Nov	Dec
Harvest	**Jan**	**Feb**	**Mar**	April	May	June	**July**	**Aug**	**Sep**	**Oct**	**Nov**	**Dec**

Rhubarb

	Jan	Feb	Mar	April	May	June	July	Aug	Sep	Oct	Nov	Dec
Sow	**Jan**	**Feb**	Mar	April	May	June	July	Aug	Sep	**Oct**	**Nov**	**Dec**
Harvest	Jan	**Feb**	**Mar**	**April**	**May**	**June**	**July**	**Aug**	Sep	Oct	Nov	Dec

Spinach

	Jan	Feb	Mar	April	May	June	July	Aug	Sep	Oct	Nov	Dec
Sow	Jan	**Feb**	**Mar**	**April**	May	June	**July**	**Aug**	**Sep**	Oct	Nov	Dec
Harvest	**Jan**	Feb	Mar	**April**	**May**	**June**	**July**	Aug	Sep	**Oct**	**Nov**	**Dec**

Flower plants

Artichoke (globe)

	Jan	Feb	Mar	April	May	June	July	Aug	Sep	Oct	Nov	Dec
Sow	Jan	Feb	Mar	April	**May**	June	July	Aug	Sep	Oct	Nov	Dec
Harvest	Jan	Feb	Mar	April	May	June	July	Aug	**Sep**	**Oct**	**Nov**	**Dec**

Broccoli

	Jan	Feb	Mar	April	May	June	July	Aug	Sep	Oct	Nov	Dec
Sow	Jan	**Feb**	**Mar**	**April**	**May**	**June**	**July**	Aug	Sep	Oct	Nov	Dec
Harvest	Jan	Feb	**Mar**	**April**	**May**	**June**	**July**	**Aug**	**Sep**	**Oct**	**Nov**	Dec

Cauliflower

	Jan	Feb	Mar	April	May	June	July	Aug	Sep	Oct	Nov	Dec
Sow	**Jan**	**Feb**	**Mar**	**April**	**May**	**June**	July	Aug	Sep	Oct	Nov	Dec
Harvest	Jan	Feb	**Mar**	**April**	**May**	**June**	**July**	**Aug**	**Sep**	**Oct**	**Nov**	Dec

Flower bulbs

	Jan	Feb	Mar	April	May	June	July	Aug	Sep	Oct	Nov	Dec
Sow	Jan	Feb	Mar	April	May	June	July	**Aug**	**Sep**	**Oct**	**Nov**	**Dec**
Harvest	Jan	**Feb**	**Mar**	**April**	**May**	**June**	July	Aug	Sep	Oct	Nov	Dec

Flowers, flowery herbs

	Jan	Feb	Mar	April	May	June	July	Aug	Sep	Oct	Nov	Dec
Sow	Jan	Feb	Mar	April	May	June	July	**Aug**	**Sep**	**Oct**	**Nov**	**Dec**
Harvest	**Jan**	**Feb**	**Mar**	**April**	**May**	**June**	**July**	**Aug**	Sep	Oct	Nov	Dec

Rose

	Jan	Feb	Mar	April	May	June	July	Aug	Sep	Oct	Nov	Dec
Sow	**Jan**	**Feb**	**Mar**	April	May	June	July	Aug	Sep	Oct	**Nov**	**Dec**
Harvest	Jan	Feb	Mar	April	**May**	**June**	**July**	**Aug**	**Sep**	**Oct**	Nov	Dec

Sunflower

	Jan	Feb	Mar	April	May	June	July	Aug	Sep	Oct	Nov	Dec
Sow	Jan	**Feb**	**Mar**	**April**	**May**	**June**	July	Aug	Sep	Oct	Nov	Dec
Harvest	Jan	Feb	Mar	April	**May**	**June**	**July**	**Aug**	**Sep**	**Oct**	**Nov**	**Dec**

Fruit plants

Aubergine (eggplant)

	Jan	Feb	Mar	April	May	June	July	Aug	Sep	Oct	Nov	Dec
Sow	**Jan**	**Feb**	**Mar**	April	May	June	July	Aug	Sep	Oct	Nov	Dec
Harvest	Jan	Feb	Mar	April	May	June	**July**	**Aug**	**Sep**	**Oct**	Nov	Dec

Barley *see* Grain

Beans, lentils

	Jan	Feb	Mar	April	May	June	July	Aug	Sep	Oct	Nov	Dec
Sow	Jan	Feb	Mar	April	**May**	**June**	**July**	Aug	Sep	Oct	Nov	Dec
Harvest	Jan	Feb	Mar	April	May	June	**July**	**Aug**	**Sep**	**Oct**	Nov	Dec

Corn *see* Maize

Courgette (zucchini)

	Jan	Feb	Mar	April	May	June	July	Aug	Sep	Oct	Nov	Dec
Sow	Jan	Feb	**Mar**	**April**	**May**	**June**	July	Aug	Sep	Oct	Nov	Dec
Harvest	Jan	Feb	Mar	April	May	**June**	**July**	**Aug**	**Sep**	**Oct**	Nov	Dec

Cucumber

	Jan	Feb	Mar	April	May	June	July	Aug	Sep	Oct	Nov	Dec
Sow	Jan	Feb	**Mar**	**April**	**May**	**June**	July	Aug	Sep	Oct	Nov	Dec
Harvest	Jan	Feb	Mar	April	May	**June**	**July**	**Aug**	**Sep**	**Oct**	Nov	Dec

Eggplant see **Aubergine**

Grains (wheat, barley, rye, oats, etc.)

Sow	Jan	Feb	Mar	April	May	**June**	**July**	**Aug**	**Sep**	Oct	Nov	Dec
Harvest	**Jan**	**Feb**	**Mar**	**April**	**May**	June	July	Aug	**Sep**	**Oct**	**Nov**	**Dec**

Maize (corn, sweetcorn)

Sow	Jan	Feb	**Mar**	**April**	**May**	**June**	July	Aug	Sep	Oct	Nov	Dec
Harvest	Jan	Feb	Mar	April	May	June	**July**	**Aug**	**Sep**	**Oct**	**Nov**	**Dec**

Melon

Sow	Jan	**Feb**	**Mar**	**April**	May	June	July	Aug	Sep	Oct	Nov	Dec
Harvest	Jan	Feb	Mar	April	May	June	**July**	**Aug**	**Sep**	Oct	Nov	Dec

Oats see **Grain**

Paprika, chilli and sweet pepper

Sow	**Jan**	**Feb**	**Mar**	April	May	June	July	Aug	Sep	Oct	Nov	Dec
Harvest	Jan	Feb	Mar	April	May	June	**July**	**Aug**	**Sep**	**Oct**	Nov	Dec

Pea

Sow	**Jan**	**Feb**	**Mar**	**April**	**May**	June	July	Aug	Sep	**Oct**	**Nov**	**Dec**
Harvest	Jan	Feb	**Mar**	**April**	**May**	**June**	**July**	Aug	Sep	Oct	Nov	Dec

Pumpkin see **Squash**

Runner bean (pole bean)

Sow	Jan	Feb	Mar	April	**May**	**June**	**July**	Aug	Sep	Oct	Nov	Dec
Harvest	Jan	Feb	Mar	April	May	June	**July**	**Aug**	**Sep**	**Oct**	Nov	Dec

Rye see **Grain**

Soya

Sow	Jan	Feb	Mar	**April**	**May**	**June**	July	Aug	Sep	Oct	Nov	Dec
Harvest	Jan	Feb	Mar	April	**May**	**June**	**July**	**Aug**	**Sep**	**Oct**	**Nov**	**Dec**

Squash (pumpkin)

Sow	Jan	Feb	**Mar**	**April**	**May**	**June**	July	Aug	Sep	Oct	Nov	Dec
Harvest	Jan	Feb	Mar	April	May	**June**	**July**	**Aug**	**Sep**	**Oct**	Nov	Dec

Strawberry

Sow	Jan	Feb	Mar	April	May	June	July	**Aug**	**Sep**	**Oct**	Nov	Dec
Harvest	Jan	Feb	Mar	**April**	**May**	**June**	**July**	**Aug**	**Sep**	Oct	Nov	Dec

Sweetcorn see **Maize**

Tomato

Sow	Jan	**Feb**	**Mar**	**April**	May	June	July	Aug	Sep	Oct	Nov	Dec
Harvest	Jan	Feb	Mar	April	May	**June**	**July**	**Aug**	**Sep**	**Oct**	Nov	Dec

Wheat see **Grain**

Zucchini see **Courgette**

Companion planting

Plants grown in close proximity influence each other, and the technique of companion planting is sometimes used for pest control, pollination or simply maximising space. For instance, leeks keep away carrot flies and carrots discourage leek moths.

Maria Thun was sceptical about companion planting, as the plants grown together are often different types (leeks are Leaf plants and carrots are Root plants). When trying to enhance their growth through the activity of hoeing and general care of the plants at Leaf or Root times, it is impossible to do justice to both plants. One or the other crop will suffer. Therefore work should be done on prime crops at times that are most beneficial to them.

The following table (based on Philbrick & Gregg, *Companion Plants*) shows which plants help vegetable, fruit, cereal and herb crops to thrive by encouraging growth, deterring pests or preventing disease.

Prime crop
  Companion crops
	Prime crop
	  Companion crops

Apple tree
  chive, nasturtium, vetch, wallflower
	Broccoli (*see also* Cabbage)
	  beetroot (beet), nasturtium

Asparagus
  parsley, tomato
	Cabbage, Brussels sprout, kale
	  beetroot (beet), camomile, celery, dill, hyssop, lettuce, mint, potato, rosemary, sage, thyme

Aubergine (eggplant) green (bush) bean	

Bean (all types)
  beetroot (beet), cabbage, carrot, cauliflower, corn (maize), cucumber, marigold, potato
	Carrot
	  chive, leek, lettuce, onion, radish, rosemary, sage

	Cauliflower (*see also* Cabbage) celery

Bean, broad (fava)
  corn (maize), oat, potato
	Celeriac
	  leek

Bean, green (bush)
  cabbage, celery, corn (maize), cucumber, potato, strawberry, summer savory
	Celery
	  green (bush) bean, leek, onion tomato

	Chervil radish, yarrow

Bean, runner (pole)
  corn (maize), radish
	Citrus tree
	  guava, live (evergreen) oak, rubber tree

Beets, beetroot cabbage, green (bush) bean, lettuce, kohlrabi, onion	

Prime crop *Companion crops*	Prime crop *Companion crops*
Corn (maize) bean, cucumber, pea, potato, wheat	**Potato** bean (except butter bean/lima), cabbage, corn, dead nettle (henbit), flax, horseradish, marigold, nasturtium, pea, sainfoin (esparcet)
Cucumber cabbage, celeriac, corn, green (bush) bean, kohlrabi, lettuce, potato, radish, sunflower	**Radish** chervil, lettuce, kohlrabi, nasturtium, pea, runner (pole) bean
Fruit tree chive, garlic, horseradish, legumes, mustard, nasturtium, stinging nettle, tansy, vetch	**Rosemary** sage, yarrow
Garlic rose	**Rye** pansy, vetch
Grapevine elm tree, hyssop, legumes, mulberry, mustard	**Sage** rosemary, yarrow
Herbs stinging nettle, yarrow	**Spinach** strawberry
Kale *see* Cabbage	**Squash (pumpkin)** corn (maize), nasturtium
Kohlrabi (*see also* Cabbage) beetroot (beet), lettuce, onion	**Strawberry** borage, green (bush) bean, lettuce, spinach
Leek carrot, celeriac, celery	**Tomato** asparagus, celery, marigold, parsley, stinging nettle
Lettuce beetroot (beet), cabbage, camomile, carrot, strawberry	**Turnip, swede (rutabaga)** pea
Melon corn (maize)	**Wheat** corn (maize), sainfoin (esparcet)
Oat vetch	
Onion beetroot (beet), carrot, celery, lettuce, summer savory	Border plants that benefit **most vegetables:** bean, borage, camomile, chervil, chive, dead nettle (henbit), dill, lavender, hyssop, lovage, marjoram, parsley, pea, sage, sainfoin (esparcet), tarragon, thyme, valerian, hyssop, lemon balm, yarrow (not fennel or wormwood)
Pea bean, carrot, cucumber, radish, potato, corn (maize), turnip/swede (rutabaga)	
Peach tree tansy	

Biodynamic preparations

The compost preparations

The classic preparation plants used by biodynamic practitioners for compost preparations are picked, dried and inserted into animal sheaths (skull, bladder, etc.). For more see Further Reading, p. 95.

- Pick *dandelions* in the morning at Flower times as soon as they are open, while the centre of the flowers are still tightly packed.
- Pick *yarrow* at Fruit times when the Sun is in Leo (around the middle of August).
- Pick *camomile* at Flower times just before midsummer. If they are harvested too late, seeds will begin to form and there are often grubs in the hollow heads.
- Collect *stinging nettles* when the first flowers are opening, usually around midsummer. Harvest the whole plants without roots at Flower times.
- Pick *valerian* at Flower times around midsummer.
- Collect *oak bark* at Root times. The pithy material below the bark should not be used.

All the flowers (except valerian) should be laid out on paper and dried in the shade.

Maria Thun's tree log preparations

Many of the classic biodynamic preparations require the use of animal organs. With the onset of BSE, using them became more difficult. This led Maria Thun to develop preparations using the bark of trees instead. They are not counted among the biodynamic preparations developed by Rudolf Steiner, but they do build on indications gained through his approach and can be used in biodynamic agriculture.

The plants should be picked and dried as indicated above. The logs for the bark need to be cut, filled and buried in the ground in accordance with lunar and planetary rhythms. These times (indicated in the calendar) need to be kept with some precision otherwise the preparations may be less effective. Since these planetary constellations do not occur regularly and in some years do not arise at all, it is worth making sufficient preparations to last more than one year. They should be stored like all biodynamic preparations, in pots surrounded by peat.

The spray preparations

There are two spray preparations – horn manure and horn silica. Maria Thun's research showed the best times to apply these.

Horn manure is most effective when sprayed on the soil, not on the plants, and is applied three times: before sowing, during sowing and after sowing. Its effect is to help the seeds and young seedlings to orientate themselves better in the soil.

Horn silica is best sprayed at Fruit times on crops beginning to shoot and form ears. Its effect is to enhance the vitality of the plant. Like horn manure, it must be stirred for a whole hour but is then only effective for up to four hours. This means that it must be sprayed out as soon as possible after stirring. The best time for spraying is immediately after sunrise, so that entails an early start.

Animal and insect pests, fungal problems

When dealing with the often significant issue of animal or insect pests, there is generally no need to reach for biological and chemical pesticides. The first step is to familiarise yourself with the conditions and habits of the pest, and to rectify any management errors that have been made. If despite this, the pest continues, it can be contained within its natural limits by using the ashes of its own burnt remains.

Snails and slugs

For an average infestation, collect between fifty and sixty animals. When the Moon is in Cancer put them in a bucket of water filled to the brim with a close fitting lid. Let it stand for four weeks until the Moon is again in Cancer, then spray the liquid where slugs and snails are a problem. Where slugs and snails are a huge problem, add some

One species, the Great Grey or Leopard Slug (Limex maximus) should be encouraged, as it feeds primarily on decaying plant remains and on the eggs of other slugs. This rare slug is 10–18 cm (4–7 in) long and unlike other large brown slugs, it is only active at night.

twenty slugs are to the horn silica preparation and stir it for an hour before spraying over the affected ground where slugs and snails are wont to feed. The light effect of silica is very disagreeable to slugs. Spray three times successively.

Mice, other mammals, birds and insects

Take a few skins of mammals, a few bird feathers, or for insects take 50 or 60 insects. Burn them in a wood fire (don't use grilling charcoal) during the appropriate planetary aspect, indicated in the 'Control pests' notes on the calendar pages. Ensure the fire is glowing hot. Lay dry feathers, skins or dead pests on the embers. After they have cooled, collect the light grey ash and grind for an hour with a pestle and mortar, as this increases its efficacy. The burning and grinding should be completed within the time indicated under Pest Control.

The ashes can be kept in an airtight jar until you need them. Label the jar with type of ash, potency and date.

The ground-up ash can then be potentised (diluted) later.

To make a liquid for spraying, place one gram (or level teaspoon) of this ground-up ash in a small bottle with 9 ml (grams, or teaspoons) of water and shake vigorously for three minutes. This is the first decimal potency (D1 or X1). Add a further 90 ml of water and shake again for three minutes. This is the second decimal potency, D2 or X2. Repeating this procedure until D8 (X8) would produce 100,000 litres (26,000 gallons). It is therefore advisable to proceed until D4 and then start again using smaller quantities (always diluting in the ratio of 1 to 9).

Alternatively the ground-up ash can be diluted with pure wood ash to make a dry ash 'pepper' for spreading on the affected area. Instead of diluting and shaking with water, use wood ash in the same proportions as water above, to make a D8 potency.

Burning skins in a wood oven

Burning in the field

Grinding the ash

Apply the liquid version as a fine mist for three evenings in succession, either using a backpack sprayer, or for large areas using a tractor-mounted sprayer. For the dry version a simple peppershaker can be used for very small areas. For larger areas, use a sowing machine with a piece of rolled-up paper set in the machine to ensure that only a minute amount of ash is released at a time).

Maria Thun advised the D8 potency was as effective as the undiluted ground-up ash, but had the advantage that a far larger area could be treated. In comparative farm trials, in both cases the animal pests remained away from the cultivated fields. The effect of deer ash could be clearly observed on an unfenced clover field where the deer had grazed the clover in the surrounding fields but not within 2 metres (7 ft) of the trial area.

Where pests occur in large numbers good results are obtained by burning them on the site where they have been found. Flea beetle and apple blossom weevil can be caught with fly papers for example and burnt on site.

Fungal problems

The function of fungus in nature is to break down dying organic materials. It appears amongst our crops when unripe manure compost or uncomposted animal by-products such as horn and bone meal are used, but also when seeds are harvested during unfavourable constellations: according to Steiner, 'When Moon forces are working too strongly on the Earth.'

Tea can be made from horsetail (*Equisetum arvense*) and sprayed on to the soil where affected plants are growing. This draws the fungal level back down into the ground where it belongs.

The plants can be strengthened by spraying stinging nettle tea on the leaves. This will promote good assimilation, stimulate the flow of sap and help fungal diseases to disappear.

Sowing and felling times for trees and shrubs

Sowing times

We can calculate optimal times for sowing seeds by looking at the Moon's position in the zodiac, depending on the part of the tree or shrub to be enhanced. You can use this method for any trees and shrubs not mentioned here. Sowing times shown here depend on planetary aspects that encourage vitality of the species; they are not specific to either northern or southern hemispheres or to any climatic region. Avoid unfavourable times.

Note: sowing times are different from Transplanting Times. Seedlings should be transplanted during the descending Moon (also called Transplanting Time) when the Moon is in a constellation corresponding to the part of the tree to to be enhanced. It is important to remember that seedlings need to be sufficiently mature to withstand the winter. The time of sowing should therefore be adapted to local conditions and take account of the germination habit of each tree species.

*Alder, **Apricot**, Elm, **Larch**, **Peach**:*
  July 17 20^h to July 18 13^h
  July 30 19^h to July 31 12^h
  Aug 20 21^h to Aug 21 14^h *(also Magnolia)*
  Sep 2 15^h to Sep 3 8^h
  Sep 18 12^h to Sep 19 5^h
  Oct 12 9^h to 13^h
  Nov 29 10^h to Nov 30 3^h.

*Apple, **Apricot**, Copper beech, Damson, Maple, Olive, **Peach**, **Sweet chestnut**, Walnut:*
  Sep 2 15^h to Sep 3 8^h
  Sep 18 12^h to Sep 19 5^h
  Sep 26 8^h to Sep 27 1^h
  Oct 12 9^h to 13^h.

*Ash, **Cedar**, Fir, Hazel, **Mirabelle plum**, Rowan, **Spruce**:*
  July 19 14^h to July 20 7^h
  Aug 14 6^h to 23^h *(also Hawthorn)*
  Sep 16 11^h to Sep 17 4^h
  Sep 26 8^h to Sep 27 1^h
  Dec 7 19^h to Dec 8 1^h & 7^h to 12^h.

*Beech, **Cedar**, Fir, Hornbeam, Juniper, Palm, Pine, Plum, Quince, Sloe, **Spruce**, Thuja:*
  July 30 19^h to July 31 12^h
  Aug 14 6^h to 23^h
  Aug 28 7^h to 24^h.

*Birch, **Larch**, Lime tree, **Mirabelle plum**, Pear, Robinia, Willow:*
  Aug 8 18^h to Aug 9 11^h
  Aug 28 7^h to 24^h
  Sep 23 22^h to Sep 24 15^h *(also Magnolia);*
  Nov 5 11^h to Nov 6 4^h
  Nov 30 18^h to Dec 1 11^h.

Blackcurrant:
  Nov 5 11^h to Nov 6 4^h.

*Cherry, Chestnut, Horse chestnut (Buckeye), Oak, **Sweet chestnut**, Yew:*
  Nov 29 10^h to Nov 30 3^h
  Nov 30 18^h to Dec 1 11^h
  Dec 7 19^h to Dec 8 1^h & 7^h to 12^h.

Lilac, Poplar, Sallow, Snowberry:
  Nov 5 11^h to Nov 6 4^h.

Note: some species (marked in **bold**) appear in two groups.

Felling times

The quality and durability of cut timber can be affected by the felling time. The dates below show optimum times for different groups of trees.

If a large number of these trees need to be felled in a short time, use the time indicated to cut the bark all around the trunk to stop sap flow. The actual felling can be done later.

Trees which are not listed should be felled at the end of the growing season at Flower times. Avoid unfavourable times.

Note that some species (marked in **bold**) appear in two groups.

*Alder, **Apricot**, Elm, **Larch**, **Peach**:*
April 28 6^h to 15^h
May 25 16^h to May 26 4^h
June 10 15^h to 24^h
July 2 5^h to 14^h
July 17 2^h to 11^h *(also Magnolia)*;
July 23 6^h to 24^h
Aug 16 7^h to 21^h
Aug 22 16^h to Aug 23 1^h
Sep 27 7^h to 16^h
Oct 6 22^h to Oct 7 7^h
Oct 22 19^h to Oct 23 4^h
Oct 26 16^h to Oct 27 7^h
Nov 12 13^h to 22^h *(also Magnolia)*
Nov 16 4^h to 22^h
Dec 17 16^h to Dec 18 1^h.

*Apple, **Apricot**, Copper beech, Damson, Maple, Olive, **Peach**, **Sweet chestnut**, Walnut:*
July 23 6^h to 24^h
July 31 10^h to 16^h
Aug 17 20^h to Aug 18 6^h
Nov 14 22^h to Nov 15 16^h
Nov 16 4^h to 22^h.

*Ash, **Cedar**, **Fir**, Hazel, **Mirabelle plum**, Rowan, **Spruce**:*
May 19 6^h to 15^h
June 16 1^h to 10^h;
July 17 17^h to July 18 2^h
July 31 10^h to 16^h
Sep 11 7^h to 16^h
Sep 18 22^h to Sep 19 7^h
Oct 17 10^h to Oct 18 1^h
Nov 14 22^h to Nov 15 7^h.

*Beech, **Cedar**, **Fir**, Hornbeam, Juniper, Palm, Pine, Plum, Quince, **Spruce**, Thuja:*
June 16 1^h to 10^h;
July 2 5^h to 14^h
Sep 28 0^h to 9^h
Oct 13 23^h to Oct 14 9^h
Oct 22 19^h to Oct 23 4^h
Nov 28 6^h to 21^h.

*Birch, **Larch**, Lime tree, **Mirabelle plum**, Pear, Robinia, Willow:*
June 21 1^h to 11^h
Aug 7 10^h to 20^h *(also Magnolia)*
Aug 17 20^h to Aug 18 6^h
Sep 19 22^h to Sep 20 8^h
Sep 25 23^h to Sep 26 9^h;
Oct 13 23^h to Oct 14 9^h
Nov 10 5^h to 15^h *(also Magnolia)*
Nov 14 22^h to Nov 15 16^h
Dec 22 3^h to 13^h.

*Cherry, Chestnut, Horse chestnut (Buckeye), Oak, **Sweet chestnut**, Yew:*
Feb 8 3^h to 18^h
Aug 14 9^h to 24^h
Sep 28 0^h to 9^h
Oct 17 10^h to Oct 18 1^h
Oct 26 16^h to Oct 27 7^h
Nov 28 6^h to 21^h.

Poplar, Sallow:
Aug 16 7^h to 21^h
Sep 19 22^h to Sep 20 8^h
Dec 17 16^h to Dec 18 1^h
Dec 22 3^h to 13^h.

Beekeeping

Bees are also influenced by the movement of the Moon. By opening and closing the beehive or skep in rhythm with the Moon, the beekeeper can directly affect the bees' activity. A beekeeping panel is shown on relevant calendar pages.

Constellation	Sign	Element (Type)	Bees	Weather tendency
Pisces	♓	Water (Leaf)	Making honey	Damp
Aries	♈	Warmth (Fruit)	Gathering nectar	Warm/hot
Taurus	♉	Earth (Root)	Building comb	Cool/cold
Gemini	♊	Light (Flower)	Gathering pollen	Airy/bright
Cancer	♋	Water (Leaf)	Making honey	Damp
Leo	♌	Warmth (Fruit)	Gathering nectar	Warm/hot
Virgo	♍	Earth (Root)	Building comb	Cool/cold
Libra	♎	Light (Flower)	Gathering pollen	Airy/bright
Scorpio	♏	Water (Leaf)	Making honey	Damp
Sagittarius	♐	Warmth (Fruit)	Gathering nectar	Warm/hot
Capricorn	♑	Earth (Root)	Building comb	Cool/cold
Aquarius	♒	Light (Flower)	Gathering pollen	Airy/bright

The care of bees

A colony of bees lives in its hive closed off from the outside world. For extra protection against harmful influences, the inside of the hive is sealed with propolis. The link with the wider surroundings is made by the bees that fly in and out of the hive.

To make good use of cosmic rhythms, the beekeeper needs to create the right conditions in much the same way as the gardener or farmer does with the plants. The gardener works the soil and in so doing allows cosmic forces to penetrate it via the air. These forces can then be taken up and used by the plants until the soil is next moved.

When the beekeeper opens up the hive, the sealing layer of propolis is broken. This creates a disturbance, as a result of which lunar and planetary forces can influence the life of the hive until the next intervention by the beekeeper. By this means the beekeeper can directly mediate cosmic forces to the bees.

It is not insignificant which forces of the universe are brought into play when the hive is opened. The beekeeper can consciously intervene by choosing days for working with the hive that will help the colony to develop and build up its food reserves. The bees will then reward the beekeeper by providing a portion of their harvest in the form of honey.

- *Earth-Root* times can be selected for opening the hive if the bees need to do more building.
- *Light-Flower* times encourage brood activity and colony development.
- *Warmth-Fruit* times stimulate the collection of nectar.
- *Water-Leaf* times are unsuitable for working in the hive or for the removal and processing of honey.

Varroa

Since the late 1970s the varroa mite has affected virtually every bee colony in Europe. Following a number of comparative trials Maria Thun recommend burning and making an ash of the varroa mite (as described on pp. 74f). After dynamising it for one hour, the ash should be put in a salt cellar and sprinkled lightly between the combs. The ash should be made and sprinkled when the Sun and Moon are in Taurus (May/June).

To strengthen the brood, small amounts of ash can also be sprinkled on the brood whenever an inspection is carried out .

Spraying the varroa ash using a salt cellar

Further reading

Berrevoets, Erik, *Wisdom of Bees: Principles of Biodynamic Beekeeping,* SteinerBooks, USA

Colquhoun, Margaret and Axel Ewald, *New Eyes for Plants,* Hawthorn

Karlsson, Britt & Per, *Biodynamic, Organic and Natural Winemaking,* Floris

Keyserlink, Adalbert Count von, *The Birth of a New Agriculture,* Temple Lodge

—, *Developing Biodynamic Agriculture,* Temple Lodge

Klett, Manfred, *Principles of Biodynamic Spray and Compost Preparations,* Floris

Klocek, Dennis, *Sacred Agriculture: The Alchemy of Biodynamics,* Lindisfarne

Koepf, H.H., *The Biodynamic Farm: Agriculture in the Service of Humanity,* SteinerBooks, USA

—, *Koepf's Practical Biodynamics: Soil, Compost, Sprays and Food Quality,* Floris

König, Karl, *Social Farming: Healing Humanity and the Earth,* Floris

Kranich, Ernst Michael, *Planetary Influences upon Plants,* Biodynamic Association, USA

Lepetit, Antoine, *What's so Special About Biodynamic Wine?* Floris

Masson, Pierre, *A Biodynamic Manual,* Floris

Morrow, Joel, *Vegetable Gardening for Organic and Biodynamic Growers,* Lindisfarne

Osthaus, K.-E., *The Biodynamic Farm,* Floris

Pfeiffer, Ehrenfried, *The Earth's Face,* Lanthorn

—, *Pfeiffer's Introduction to Biodynamics,* Floris

—, *Weeds and What They Tell Us,* Floris

—, & Michael Maltas, *The Biodynamic Orchard Book,* Floris

Philbrick, John & Helen, *Gardening for Health and Nutrition,* Anthroposophic, USA

Philbrick, Helen & Gregg, Richard B., *Companion Plants: An A to Z for Gardeners and Farmers,* Floris

Sattler, Friedrich & Eckard von Wistinghausen, *Growing Biodynamic Crops,* Floris

Selg, Peter, *The Agricultural Course: Rudolf Steiner and the Beginnings of Biodynamics,* Temple Lodge

Steiner, Rudolf, *Agriculture (A Course of Eight Lectures),* Biodynamic Association, USA (also published in another translation by Rudolf Steineer Press, UK)

—, *Agriculture: An Introductory Reader,* Steiner Press, UK

—, *What is Biodynamics? A Way to Heal and Revitalize the Earth,* SteinerBooks, USA

Storl, Wolf, *Culture and Horticulture,* North Atlantic Books, USA

Thun, Maria, *Gardening for Life,* Hawthorn

—, *The Biodynamic Year,* Temple Lodge

Thun, Matthias, *Biodynamic Beekeeping,* Floris

Weiler, Michael, *The Secret of Bees: An Insider's Guide to the Life of the Honeybee,* Floris

Wright, Hilary, *Biodynamic Gardening for Health and Taste,* Floris

Biodynamic associations

Demeter International
www.demeter.net
Australia:
Australian Demeter Bio-Dynamic
demeterbiodynamic.com.au/
Biodynamic Agriculture Australia
www.biodynamics.net.au
Canada (Ontario): Society for Bio-Dynamic
Farming & Gardening in Ontario
biodynamics.on.ca   (see also USA)
India: Bio-Dynamic Association of
India (BDAI)
www.biodynamics.in

Ireland: Biodynamic Agriculture Association
of Ireland
www.biodynamicagriculture.ie
New Zealand:
NZ Biodynamic Association
www.biodynamic.org.nz
South Africa: Biodynamic Agricultural
Association of Southern Africa
www.bdaasa.org.za
UK: Biodynamic Association
www.biodynamic.org.uk
USA: Biodynamic Assoc. of North America
www.biodynamics.com

Moon diagrams

The diagrams overleaf show for each month the daily position (evenings GMT) of the Moon against the stars and other planets. For viewing in the southern hemisphere, turn the diagrams upside down.

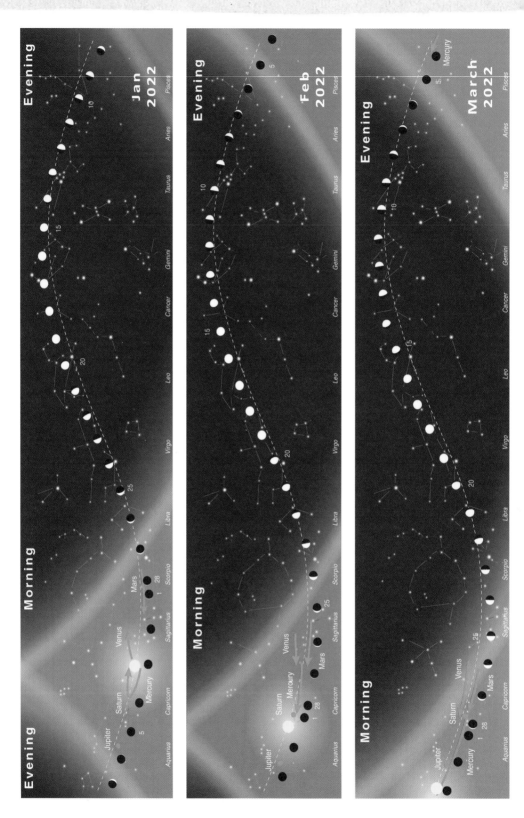

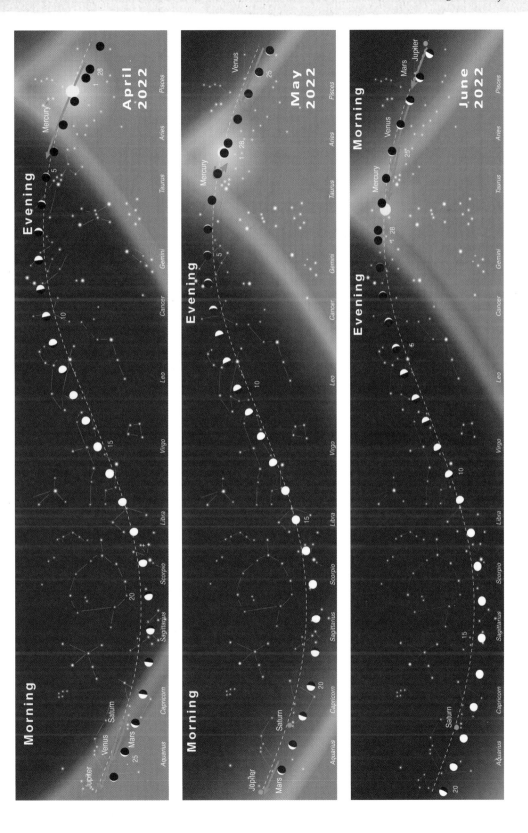

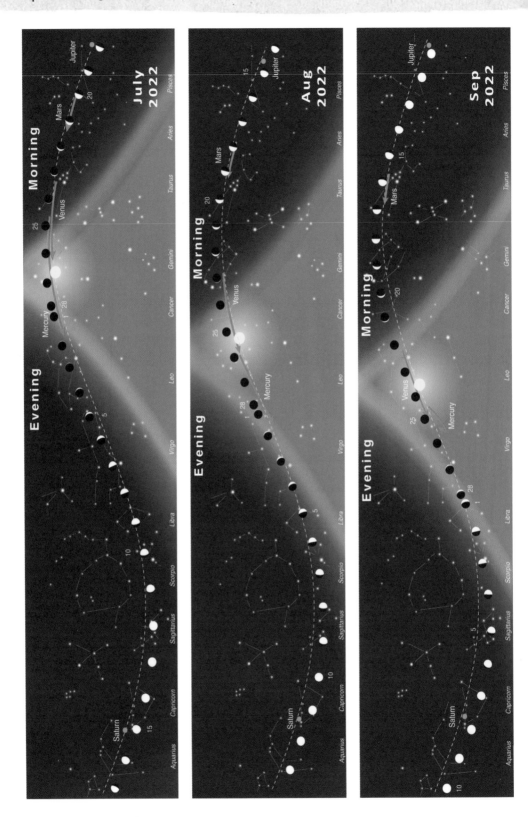

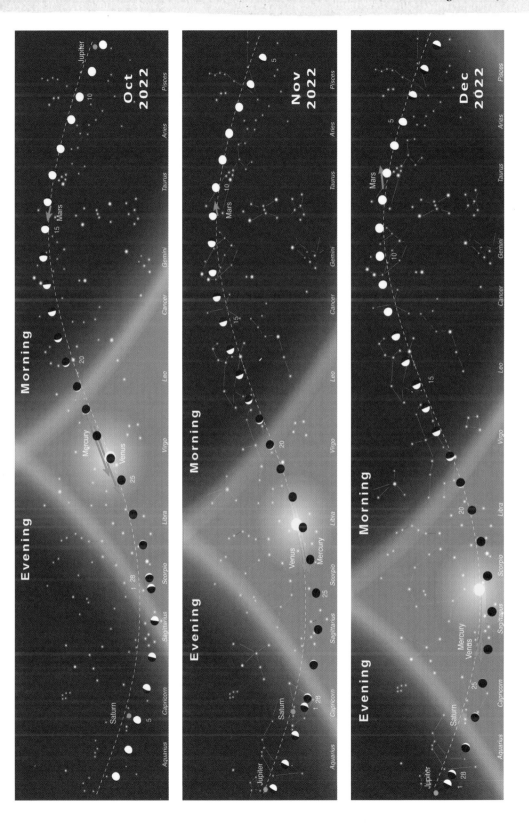

In memory of Matthias Thun

Titia Thun

On June 22, 2020, our dear father, Matthias Kaspar Thun, passed away quite unexpectedly.

At 72 he might not have been a young man, but he was still full of life. He enjoyed watching my brother, Friedrich, take over the farm here in Dexbach and supported him with all his power in this endeavour. In his last year he was able to find pleasure in new animals here, revived many old friendships, finally put down old arguments and also rekindled his relationship to nature with a new passion. His sudden death was therefore a surprise and a shock for us.

Matthias was born in Marburg, Germany, on Sunday February 29, 1948. Again and again he proudly told us that only children who are born on this date of a leap year, and also on a Sunday, are able to find treasure. According to local legend only they are given the gift to see the golden spinning wheel in the River Lahn. Matthias may not have found exactly this spinning wheel, but he was convinced that he had led a lucky life.

He dedicated most of his life to his mother's service, tending her agricultural research and supporting her with heart and soul. Without his support, she would not have been able to carry out her research and maintain a close contact with people around the world who also felt the importance of understanding how cosmic forces worked on earth. He felt obliged to continue publishing the *Maria Thun Biodynamic Calendar* after his mother died, to maintain and continue her work. When she fell ill he cared for her for to the end, as he had cared for his father before. He kept the promise he had made to his parents that they could always live and grow old with him.

My brother and I never made such a promise, and we knew we were free to do whatever we wanted to do. My brother Friedrich went into agriculture of his own accord and I made writing my vocation. However, we have been actively working with our father over the past few years, calculating the data and writing for the calendar.

We shall continue the publishing activity and we are ready to take on the task of honouring our grandmother's legacy in this way.

Friedrich (born in 1996) and I (born a year later) are both still comparatively young and even if we tried, we will of course not have the same experience that our father and our grandmother brought to the calendar. Nonetheless, Maria Thun's work will remain at the centre of this calendar – there are countless unpublished texts she wrote that will be reviewed over the coming few years. We will take up the questions that Maria Thun left us and continue to try to answer them.

Maria and Matthias Thun

Horn silica

Maria Thun

Ever since biodynamic farming has existed efforts have been made to understand the observed effects of the preparations. To find out where changes occur when the preparations are applied we must set up comparative trials. We can then see by starting from the phenomena, whether plants treated with the preparations show differences in terms of form, leaf shape or in other ways as compared to untreated plants growing under identical conditions. Some plants are more suited to this task than others. A plant that has the capacity to express significant changes in leaf form will also be capable of showing other differences – unlike grasses and cereals, for instance.

Cereals on the other hand *are* able to show variation in other areas. The form of their ears, the colour of their flowers and, in the case of follow-up cultivation, the colour of the germinating seedling. Comparisons made within the plant family can reveal more vigorous growth or at other times a reduction in vitality. If a plant is removed from the earth further information can be gleaned from the roots.

Our observations are always based on the phenomena. Another step towards understanding the effects of the preparations can be taken by using size, number and weight to confirm the differences. But this focus on quantity (higher yields) ignores the question of quality. What is quality? How can quality be measured? Simply looking healthy is not enough.

This brings us to the question of the substances contained in the plant. Are we now finally in the realm of quality or still occupied with quantity when we discover a particularly high protein or sugar content? This demonstrates the need to further unpack the concept of quality.

The plant expresses two dominant gestures – one is providing food and the other is producing seed. According to the indications given by Rudolf Steiner in the Agriculture Course, these two tendencies are the consequence of planetary effects. Food quality is enhanced when the Sun's influence is moderated by the working of Mars, Jupiter and Saturn, while Moon, Mercury and Venus enhance the reproductive power. The key question for us is, how we can stimulate the one or the other?

When taken in as food, each part of the plant influences a different area of the human being. The main substances in food are proteins, fats, carbohydrates and salts. These substances arise from life processes and are carriers of invisible forces and processes. However, they leave traces in the substances, and we can try to orientate ourselves via these traces.

When discussing the compost preparations during the Agriculture Course, Rudolf Steiner said that their effect is to enable soil and plants to take up cosmic influences more strongly. He described the subtle influences that stream from the surroundings into the soil and become available to plants. They always change whenever the soil is moved – as the extensive research into different sowing times has confirmed.

Our research into the silica (quartz) preparation shows that the connection between plant and cosmos is strengthened through the application of horn silica.

The daily rhythm

The day has a natural rhythm, which starts with an ascending period during the morning when the light grows stronger. Around midday it reaches a peak as though holding its breath. Then it declines in the afternoon. We can observe a similar activity in plants with ascending forces and rising sap in the morning. Around the hours of noon the plant does not wish to be disturbed and then in the afternoon there is a descending process. Just as in the morning the gesture is one of opening up to the cosmos followed by a kind midday sleep, in the afternoon a stronger connection with the earth is sought.

We have repeatedly observed in our trials how a morning application of the horn silica preparation strongly stimulates the upper part of the plant and the forming of substances, while an afternoon application influences root growth and encourages the fruiting process in the roots. This expresses itself with increased yields but also in changes of root form. For example, in the case of field beans we have often seen how a morning spray enhances the vertical growth tendency while an afternoon spray stimulates the root to develop more of a ball-shape which in turn expresses a fruit-forming tendency.

The plant needs to tune into the changing relationship of the Sun to the Earth during the course of the day, and this is strengthened when horn silica is applied. But this also means that an afternoon application will have a devitalising effect on the upper part of the plant and it is important to assess whether the plant can cope with such stress during that stage of growth. A morning application always enhances vitality.

If we have grain crop that is ripening too slowly and we give a morning application of horn silica, new vitalising processes are activated, which might lead to the grain sprouting in the ear. In this case it would be better to apply horn silica in the afternoon to reduce vitality. For root plants (like carrots or potatoes) we must make sure they develop enough foliage for good assimilation. Horn silica should then be applied in the morning during the early growth stages. Only once the plant above ground is fully developed should we give an afternoon spray to enhance the fruiting roots.

The monthly rhythm

With horn silica we found that not only could we enhance the effects of the daily rhythm, but also the rhythm of the Moon's passage through the zodiac, which also influences plant growth. Spraying trials showed how zodiacal influences were enhanced by the silica preparation.

We found that the effect was strongest when the spraying was carried out for:

- root crops at Root times
- leaf crops at Leaf times
- fruit crops at Fruit times

Taking account of the Moon's course through the zodiac when spraying horn silica led to an increase in yield, improved health, better germination and more vigorous seedlings. Subsequent analysis gave strong confirmation of this. Plants treated with horn silica at the right moment were often found to contain more of the trace elements required by human beings. But there were also other improvements – an improved ratio between nitrogen and sugar in spinach leaves or a more favourable protein-carbohydrate ratio in cereal grains. With roots grown for human food it is important to have the right proportion of vegetable salts and here too the best results occur when the application is made under the most favourable cosmic conditions.

Comparative spraying trials with horn silica

How often and at what time of day should we spray horn silica?

The practical question is often raised: how often should horn silica be sprayed to achieve maximum effect? Comparative trials with up to ten successive daily applications have shown that the greatest effect occurs with three or four applications. Further sprayings have no measurable effect.

Numerous trials using different rhythms on various crops have been undertaken with horn silica for more than ten years and the results described above have been confirmed time and again. Analysis of crops using visual image methods (crystallisation, chromatograms, water drop pictures) always show the presence of strong formative forces in the plant whenever horn silica had been applied. Storage tests have shown improved keeping quality.

In the case of the four cosmic influences we found that the effects of spraying at Root, Leaf, Fruit or Flower times enhanced the development of that part of the plant.

However, the effect of the silica preparation was diminished in some cases. Plants sown at Flower times and sprayed with the preparation the same day produced lower yields and revealed a hardening tendency in the visual image tests. When their seeds were sown the following year these plants again had lower yields than the control. This seemed to be a question of light. Flower times tend to have an intensive light quality. An hour after spraying, plants often turn the upper surfaces of their leaves away from the light.

At this point we must again look more closely at the time of day when the spraying took place. The reactions of the plants referred to above could, in some cases, also be observed if spraying was carried between noon and 2 pm. To determine the best time of day more precisely, spraying trials were carried out at hourly intervals from dawn till dusk. These showed that the best time for a morning application was before 9 am, and for an afternoon spray after 5 pm. These trials were carried out during long summer days.

This shows that the time of day when the Sun is at its highest is unsuitable for spraying horn silica. Applications carried out at Flower times before 7 am and after 7 pm – when the Sun is low – displayed none of the problems indicated above. It is clear that the preparation has a powerful light effect which the plant is unable to deal with when the external light is at its strongest.

Other trials clearly show that treating plants growing in the shade with the silica preparation enables them to overcome or reduce the effects of shade. Dr Heintz at the University of Strasbourg, who developed a method to show the light effect of the horn silica, has since confirmed the results that we observed in plants.

Stirring the preparation

It was uncertain how long the stirred preparation remains effective. We found through our planting trials that it works for four hours and then gradually loses its effectiveness. Dr Heintz observed something similar. He compared the horn silica preparation with a similar amount of unprepared ground-up quartz and found that the light effect of horn silica was stronger and lasted longer than the ground-up quartz.

This brings us back to the starting substance. For making horn silica preparation we use transparent rock crystal that is as free as possible from other substances. Pure quartz of this kind is used industrially for making lenses. If we take a magnifying glass, allow the Sun to shine through it and hold a paper underneath, it will catch fire and burn. The substance of silica and the way it is formed means that, like a lens, it can gather and strengthen the light and warmth effect.

We are of course not holding a lens over the plant when we use horn silica. In making the preparation we put the finely ground quartz into a cow horn. The horn's form and its spiralling tendency has a strong and concentrated effect within biological processes. It is placed into

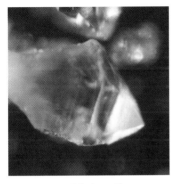

Quartz crystal (enlarged)   *Ground up 'silica sand' (enlarged)*

the earth for the whole summer, where it experiences the effect of the summer Sun and concentrates it in the preparation.

It is worth noting that Rudolf Steiner referred in his text to 'silica or quartz flour'. We must remember that in Steiner's day granules of flour were not as fine as today. In trials carried out by Maria Thun it was found that when quartz is ground as fine as flour is expected to be today, it is no longer capable of meeting the requirements of the preparation. The quality is reduced. The silica should not be ground so fine that it loses its crystalline structure. It would be better nowadays to therefore speak of fine silica sand.

We take about 5 grams (a little less than ¼ oz) of this preparation, stir it in an earthenware or wooden container for an hour in 40–50 litres (10–13 US gal) and in doing so form good vortices. This is sufficient for an area of 1 hectare (2½ acres).

Stirring should proceed from the perimeter of the container, intensifying towards the centre, and not from the centre outwards. By stirring in from the outside, layers of liquid rub against one another and draw in forces from the periphery. If we stir outward from the centre there is a dispersal and the effectiveness of the preparation is greatly reduced. The preparation's forces of light and warmth are transferred to the water.

Once stirring is completed the preparation must be sprayed within three or four hours. After that its effectiveness declines. On larger areas it is advisable to combine spraying with hoeing or harrowing; this saves a lot of time but also increases the effect of horn silica if the soil is simultaneously cultivated.

The effect on plants

Let us now return to the plant. We spray the preparation on the leaves of the plant. This seems to engender a change in the way the cells experience light. It is perhaps a kind of refraction such as we experience when, through a prism or in nature, the colours of the rainbow emerge. It appears that the differentiated effect of light on the plant calls forth a range of colours such as we often see in dew drops, which then stimulates the formation of various substances.

Depending on the cosmic influences active at the time the preparation is applied, the plant will then develop particular substances like proteins, fats, essential oils, sugars, salts or trace elements. If the light effect is too powerful the plant will not be able to cope with its intensity and cannot be creative. Something then occurs which may be compared to a certain level of burning that expresses itself in a hardening and regressive process in the plant.

For the practical application here is a brief overview:

- At *Root times* – potatoes, carrots, beetroot, etc. Spray applications in the morning during the early vigorous growth stages; later on, during the afternoon.
- At *Leaf times* – spinach, lettuce, kale, meadows, pastures, clover, etc. Spray applications in the morning or, if there is danger of bolting, in the afternoon.
- At *Flower times* – rape, buckwheat, mint, melissa, etc. Spray very early in the morning.
- At *Fruit times* – tomatoes, cucumbers, cereals, peas, beans, etc. Spray early in the morning.